MW01629279

Better Homes and Gardens®
celebrate the
SEASON®
2011

table *of* contents

celebrate autumn

page 6 Get ready to make the most of fall's lucious colors and distinctive motifs. From leaf-laden decorations to unforgettable place settings and from nature's best displays to room decor that sings with style, these ideas help blanket your home with do-it-yourself projects that look designer perfect.

deck the halls

page 32 Ring in Christmas with trims that beam with glad tidings. You'll discover fun ways to dress the table, clever ornaments to trim the tree, cozy comforts to warm your wintry home, and so much more. This chapter inspires you to make this special time of year the merriest ever.

savor the season

page 88 As you gather family and friends together this holiday season, treat them to incredible feasts from your very own kitchen. Choose from wondrous appetizers, meats, side dishes, drinks, and desserts—all the recipes you need to create that just-right menu.

give from the heart

page 120 If you like to surprise gift recipients with a little something unexpected, your best bet is to make it yourself. You're sure to find something for every good boy and girl in this chapter filled with incredible gift ideas that are as easy on the budget as they are to make.

inspire the kids

page 140 Kids who like to craft will love these projects they can do themselves. Whether they are spiffing up their room for holiday company or are making awesome gifts for family and friends, kids will discover oodles of fun make-it-yourself ideas in this kid-friendly chapter.

in a twinkling

Enjoy easy-to-make projects and quick-to-cook recipes that get nothing less than rave reviews.

- Fanciful Feathers page 30
- Bright Lights page 86
- Creative Cupcakes page 118
- Disc Disguises page 138
- Bejeweled Trims page 152

Better Homes and Gardens®

Celebrate the Season®

Meredith Corporation Consumer Marketing
Vice President, Consumer Marketing: David Ball
Consumer Product Marketing Director: Steve Swanson
Consumer Product Marketing Manager: Wendy Merical
Business Manager: Ron Clingman
Photographers: Jason Donnelly, Scott Little,
Kritsada Panichgul, Jay Wilde

Waterbury Publications, Inc.
Contributing Editor: Sue Banker
Contributing Graphic Designer: Catherine Brett
Editorial Director: Lisa Kingsley
Associate Editor: Tricia Laning
Creative Director: Ken Carlson
Associate Design Director: Doug Samuelson
Production Assistants: Kim Hopkins, Mindy Samuelson
Contributing Food Editor: Lois White
Contributing Food Stylists: Dianna Nolan, Jennifer Peterson
Contributing Copy Editor: Terri Fredrickson
Contributing Proofreaders: Gretchen Kauffman, Candy Meier

Better Homes and Gardens® **Magazine**
Editor in Chief: Gayle Goodson Butler
Art Director: Michael D. Belknap
Deputy Editor, Food and Entertaining: Nancy Wall Hopkins
Senior Food Editor: Richard Swearinger
Associate Food Editor: Erin Simpson
Editorial Assistant: Renee Irey

Meredith Publishing Group
Executive Vice President: Andy Sareyan
Vice President, Manufacturing: Bruce Heston

Meredith Corporation
Chairman of the Board: William T. Kerr
President and Chief Executive Officer: Stephen M. Lacy

Copyright © 2011 by Meredith Corporation.
Des Moines, Iowa.
First Edition. All rights reserved.
Printed in the United States of America.
ISSN: 1098-9733   ISBN: 978-0-696-30062-2

All of us at Meredith Consumer Marketing are dedicated to
providing you with information and ideas to enhance your home.
We welcome your comments and suggestions. Write to us at:
Meredith Consumer Marketing, 1716 Locust St.,
Des Moines, IA 50309-3023

Seasonal Surprises

I've always been one who likes to put a spin on things. Would I use a floral shop bouquet as a centerpiece? Only if there are goldfish swimming in the vase. Do I serve the kids a plain PB&J sandwich? Not until I cut it into fun shapes.

It's those little twists and touches that turn the ordinary into the extraordinary. And when the holidays roll around, those from-the-heart acts are what make the very best memories.

Special touches like these don't require lots of time or money to make them happen. All it takes is the desire to wear Santa's hat for awhile and create holiday magic all around you.

Celebrate the Season offers hundreds of ways to make the season merrier. If you like to dress your home with festive flair, we'll show you how. From quick little touches to total room transformations, you'll be inspired to craft yourself silly. And if you have little do-it-yourselfers, we've included kid- and family-friendly projects too.

If you like to throw a party, we have you covered. The incredibly creative tabletops and mouthwatering foods will leave guests admiring your talents and appreciating your thoughtfulness.

Or maybe you'd like to give more personal gifts this year. Look no further! You can't miss with wonderful surprises like Toffee Blondies in a jar and beautiful etched candleholders.

There's no better time than the Christmas season to unleash your creative spirit. What a generous way to show your friends and family love in this season of giving.

Wishing you a sleighful of unexpected joys at Christmas and always,

Sue Barker

CELEBRATE
AUTUMN

Let the richness of the season infuse your fall decorating with vivid color and hints of nature.

Cool Copper

Blending well with other autumnal hues, reddish orange copper is a welcome addition to the season's decorating.

Candle Cluster

■ Place neutral candles in copper containers and fill them with an assortment of pinecones, acorns, or nuts in the shell. Place the arrangement on a copper tray for a lovely autumn decoration. If lighting the candles, be sure to keep the pinecones away from the flames.

Fresh for Fall

■ A copper coffeepot serves as a beautiful unexpected vase for a fresh bouquet in autumn tones. To carry out the copper theme, coat a wired berry pick with copper acrylic paint.

Beribboned Beauty

■ Soften the surface of a copper tray with a striped ribbon mat. Cut ribbons 2 inches longer than needed to fit the tray. Use a sewing machine and zigzag stitches in copper thread to attach various colored and patterned ribbons side by side. Turn under 1 inch on each raw edge and stitch in place.

Pretty Plate

■ Give a charger a copper patina that brings metallic shine to the table. Paint the charger with spray primer and let dry. Spray on two light coats of copper-color spray paint, allowing to dry between coats. When dry, hot-glue copper-color or clear flat marbles evenly spaced around the edge. Detail the edging with copper-color metallic fiber bordering the glass pieces.

Elegant Wrap

■ Craft a coordinating napkin ring by spraying a chunky wood ring with copper paint. When dry, wrap the ring with variegated copper-color fiber. Tack the threads in place on the inside of the ring using dots of hot glue.

Grand Stand

■ Pinecones dusted with a light brushing of copper acrylic paint act as charming place card holders. Write names on small rectangular white stickers or paper and back with copper-color cardstock.

Egg-stra Special

■ Copper egg cups are just the right size for holding after-dinner sweets. Check cooking stores for these or other small copper containers that double as favors for guests.

Hip to Be Square

Honor fall with useful home accents crafted from decorative paper squares.

Box It Up

■ Small papier-mâché boxes available in crafts stores make perfect party favors. Cut scrapbooking or wrapping paper to cover the sides and coordinating paper to cover the lid. Use a glue stick to adhere the paper in place. Trim the lid edges with two rows of suede trim hot-glued in place. Glue a pinecone and a pair of suede loops on the lid.

Pretty in Plaid

■ Pick plaid paper in seasonal colors to set the tone for easy-to-make coasters. Back four 1½-inch squares with a slightly larger square of solid paper, securing squares in place with a glue stick. Back the layers with coordinating polka-dot and solid papers. To waterproof the coasters, laminate them.

Quilted Mat

■ Join 4-inch paper squares with tape on the back to create a 12-patch mat. Using the pattern on page 154, cut out three leaves from contrasting paper. Use a glue stick to adhere them on three squares. Cut fourteen 1¼-inch paper squares. On each end of place mat, set seven squares on point, overlap to fit, and tape in place. For protection, laminate the mat.

harvest
family

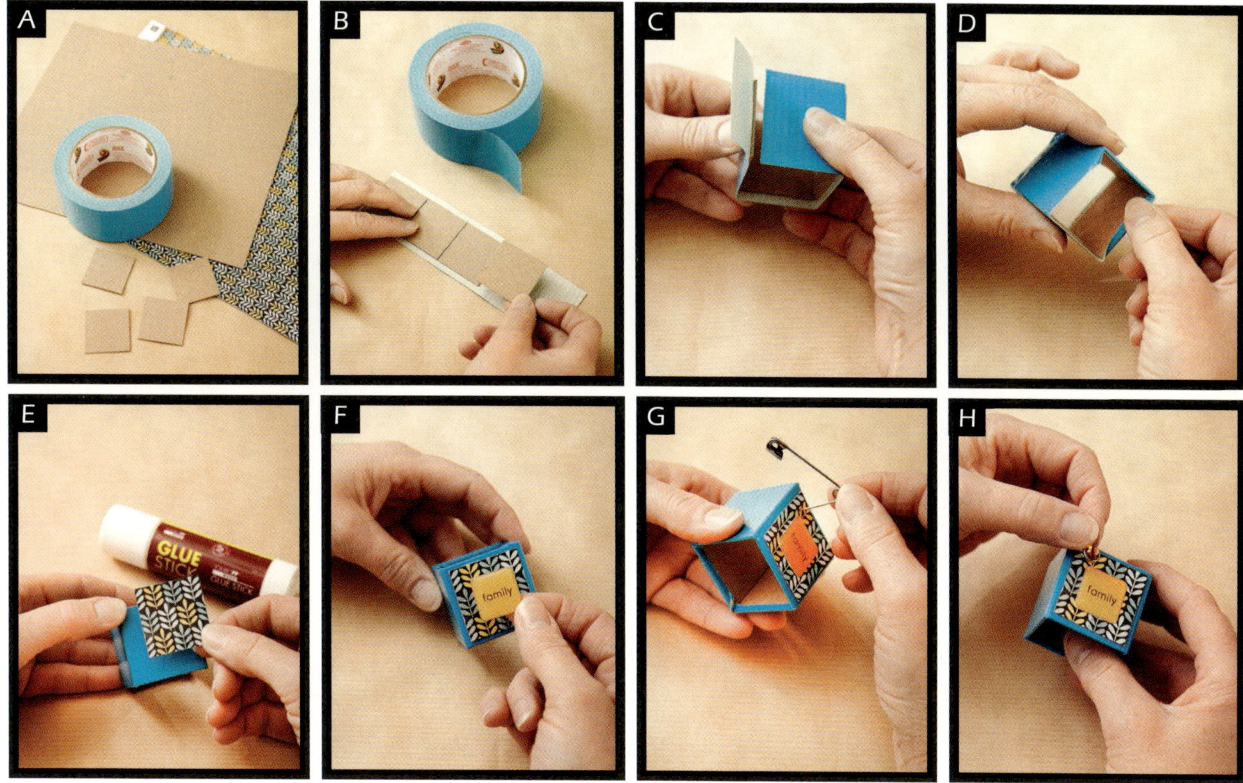

Ring Around the Napkin

■ Coordinating scrapbook supplies and duct tape lead the way to making personalized napkin rings for all the guests at the table.

- ruler
- pencil
- medium-weight cardboard
- scissors
- duct tape in turquoise or other desired color
- decorative print paper in turquoise and autumn colors
- glue stick
- 1-inch square word stickers
- large safety pin
- decorative gem-studded scrapbooking brad

1 **For each napkin ring,** use a ruler and pencil to mark four 1½-inch squares on cardboard; cut out as shown in Photo A.

2 **Cut a 7-inch-long length of duct tape.** Align 1 cardboard square centered at one end of the tape. Place the remaining 3 cardboard squares side by side on the tape next to the first square as shown in Photo B.

3 **Bring the ends of the cardboard strip together** as shown in Photo C; press the tape end over the opposite end to hold the square shape in place.

4 **Fold over the tape** to cover the cardboard edges as shown in Photo D.

5 **Use a ruler and pencil** to mark a 1¼-inch square from decorative paper; cut out. Use glue stick to adhere paper square centered on napkin ring on the side opposite from the tape seam as shown in Photo E.

6 **Adhere a sticker** centered on the paper square as shown in Photo F.

7 **Using a safety pin,** poke a hole through napkin ring ⅛ inch from upper left corner of paper as shown in Photo G.

8 **Insert decorative brad** through hole as shown in Photo H; open prongs on inside of napkin ring.

Basket Beauty

Inside or outside, hanging or sitting, natural woven baskets can hold a treasure trove of seasonal delights.

A Step Ahead

■ A stair basket filled to the brim with mums is a welcoming addition to the front porch. As a finishing touch, tie on a plaid bow in coordinating colors to the arrangement.

Earthly Bounty

■ Place Indian corn in a basket and arrange the husks as a fanfare. Tuck in a sprig of dried berries and top with a pumpkin gourd to create a focal point.

Hang It Up

■ A semicircular basket hangs on the wall with ease. Fill it with a dried arrangement and hot-glue a bow to one side to complete the autumnal accessory.

Garden Fresh

■ When the colors of summer fade, plant colorful kale in a lined basket to add interest to end-of-season gardens.

Flea
Market
Fancies
Found by the dozens at thrift shops
and flea markets, the supplies used
for these projects are easy on the
budget yet yield stunning results.

Mirror, Mirror on the Wall

■ While the scenes on brass plates may be passé, their borders hold intricate beauty. A burnished patina shows off the decorative designs that make the perfect border for a new beveled mirror.

What You'll Need

- [ ] brass plate with decorative border and wall hanger
- [ ] foam brush
- [ ] water-base glaze in dark brown, such as General Finishes VanDyke brown
- [ ] rag
- [ ] mirror adhesive
- [ ] beveled mirror to fit center of plate

1 Brush the border of the plate with a generous coat of glaze as shown in Photo A. While wet, use a rag to remove the glaze from the raised areas of the design as shown in Photo B. Let the glaze dry.

2 Apply thick dots of mirror adhesive to the center of the plate and the back of the mirror as shown in Photo C.

3 Center the mirror on the plate and press gently in place as shown in Photo D; let adhesive dry.

Pretty Plate

■ Cut-glass plates, plentiful in secondhand shops, gain an interesting punch of color with no-fail strokes of paint. Working on the plate back, paint on one or two glass paint colors for the desired look. To define the cut-glass designs, allow the crevices to remain unpainted. Let the paint dry. Follow the manufacturer's instructions for curing the paint.

Woodsy Warmth

■ Give a large chunky picture frame a new life as a table tray. Simply freshen up the wood, add a fabric insert, and edge with upholstery tacks for a handsome remodel.

- large chunky wood picture frame
- pliers (optional)
- rubber gloves; rags
- denatured alcohol
- foam paintbrush
- water-base wood stain
- spray lacquer
- yardstick
- permanent black marking pen
- upholstery tacks or decorative adhesive nail heads
- hammer
- plywood cut to fit frame
- spray adhesive for fabric
- fabric to fit plywood
- 1-inch brad nails
- felt to fit frame back
- strong adhesive for fabric and wood

1 **If necessary, remove picture** from frame as shown in Photo A.

2 **Put on rubber gloves.** Use a rag dampened with denatured alcohol to clean frame as shown in Photo B; let dry.

3 **Using a foam brush** and a small amount of stain, brush the frame surfaces with a light, even coat as shown in Photo C; let dry.

4 **In a well-ventilated area** and following the manufacturer's instructions, spray the frame with lacquer as shown in Photo D; let dry.

5 **Determine how close** to place upholstery tacks. Using a yardstick and pen, mark frame edge at even intervals. Use a hammer to carefully tap tacks into frame where marked as shown in Photo E. If the frame is not thick enough to hold tacks, press on adhesive nail heads.

6 **In a well-ventilated area,** cover the work surface. Following the manufacturer's instructions, spray adhesive onto the cut plywood as shown in Photo F. Carefully place fabric on plywood as shown in Photo G, aligning edges.

7 **Insert fabric-covered plywood** into frame. Use a hammer to tap brads into frame, holding plywood sturdily into frame as shown in Photo H.

8 **Use strong adhesive** to adhere felt to the back of the frame; let dry.

House Dresses at
Factory Prices
ROSES
Guide to Rose Culture
THE DINGEE & CONARD CO., BOX 594,
ART
AND
CRAF

Yo-Yo Cone

■ Marry yesteryear's magazine pages and fabric prints to craft a unique holder for a dried autumn arrangement.

What You'll Need

- [ ] 8-inch fabric circle cut from thrift store vintage clothing
- [ ] thread
- [ ] sewing needle
- [ ] large vintage button
- [ ] double-sided tape
- [ ] cardboard cone
- [ ] old newspaper or magazine pages
- [ ] hot-glue gun; glue sticks

1 To make a fabric yo-yo, sew a running stitch ¼ inch from the edge of the circle as shown in Photo A.

2 Gently pull the thread to gather the circle edge until there is a center hole about the size of a nickel as shown in Photo B; knot thread.

3 Sew a button in the center of the yo-yo as shown in Photo C; set aside.

4 Place a piece of double-stick tape onto cone as shown in Photo D. Wrap cone with paper, placing one edge of paper on tape to secure. Use a second piece of tape to secure remaining edge as shown in Photo E.

5 Roll a second piece of paper to act as a liner for the cone; slip it into place as shown in Photo F.

6 Hot-glue the yo-yo decoration to the side of the cone.

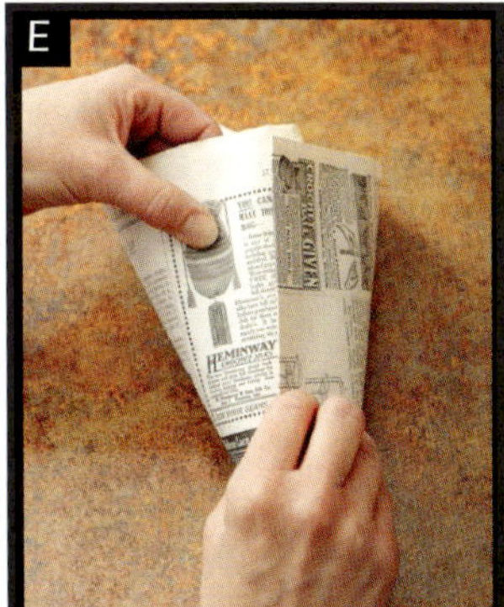

Leaf It to Nature

Leaves, so symbolic of the season, offer limitless motifs to enhance decorating.

Carved Creation

Decorate your doorstep with a longer-lasting pumpkin. Trace a maple leaf or use the pattern on page 154, then use a linoleum cutter or potter's ribbon tool to scrape out the design, being careful not to cut completely through.

Showstopper

◼ For an easy wreath, hot-glue pressed leaves around the edge of a platter and hang with a plate hook. The glue peels right off when you want to use the platter again.

Subtle Charm

◼ Label guests' wineglasses with leaf cutouts. Use fresh leaves as patterns to cut out designs from paper. Punch a small hole through each paper cutout and tie onto the glasses with gold cord.

Fall Flourish

◼ Colorful leaves and mini mums bring casual seasonality to a rose bouquet. Displaying the arrangement on a cake stand with mini pumpkins elevates its impact.

Plaid 'n' Pumpkins

■ Choose earthy plaid ribbon that coordinates with your dishes. Tie a generous bow on the stem of a pumpkin gourd, allowing the tails to trail off the plate.

Free Falling

■ Tumbled leaves in vibrant hues bring natural appeal to the table. Wash and dry leaves, then tuck them into the napkin ring along with a leaf-theme fabric napkin.

Thanks-Filled Settings

Welcome Thanksgiving guests with clever place settings suited to the special occasion.

Berried Beauty

Seasonal picks add instant elegance to the table. Avoid choosing those with glitter so dishes and napkins remain clean. Wind wire ends around a pencil or dowel to lend final polish.

What a Pear

■ A wooden napkin ring allows a fresh pear
to stand at attention atop the place setting.
Frame the grandstander with a gently knotted
fabric napkin.

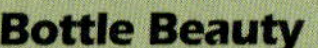

In a Twinkling
Fanciful Feathers

Pretty Place Cards

Add dimension to a paper place card by showcasing a tiny crafts store feather to one side. Use a small paper punch to make a pair of holes, thread the feather quill through, and tape on the back.

Nice Note ▶

Corrugated cardboard creates a natural backdrop to enhance a single feather. Subtle patterned papers in coordinating tones complete the designer look.

DECK *the* HALLS

Let the joy of the holiday season shine through with trims and table settings to guide you from a merry Christmas all the way to a happy New Year.

Paper Play

Head to the scrapbook paper aisle and you'll find endless design combinations to make festive holiday trims.

Festive Spheres

■ Put a new spin on these classic trims by using pretty scrapbook papers to coordinate with your holiday decorating color scheme.

What You'll Need

- [ ] 2-inch circle paper punch
- [ ] patterned scrapbook papers
- [ ] tracing paper
- [ ] pencil
- [ ] scissors
- [ ] heavy cardstock
- [ ] glue stick
- [ ] narrow ribbon (optional)
- [ ] thick crafts glue
- [ ] glitter

1 For each sphere, punch out 20 circles from papers as shown in Photo A or use pattern on page 155.

2 Trace the triangle pattern on page 155; cut out. Use the pattern to cut a triangle from heavy cardstock. Center the triangle in each circle and fold up the edges around it as shown in Photo B.

3 To make the sphere top, use a glue stick to join together 5 folded circles as shown in Photo C. To make a hanger if desired, cut a 10-inch piece of ribbon and knot the ends. From the underside of the paper circle, push the loop of the ribbon through the center and gently pull until the knot is snug to the paper as shown in Photo D.

4 Make the sphere bottom in the same manner as the top. Join the remaining 10 circles together into a long strip as shown in Photo E. Glue the strip ends together. Glue on the top and bottom.

5 Working in small sections, run a line of crafts glue along paper edges; sprinkle with glitter. Continue until all edges are covered.

Dots Galore Wreath

■ This pretty trim makes use of greeting cards from holidays past. To make the base, cut a cardstock donut shape using 2- and 3-inch circle cutters. Choose cards with green motifs to make the main part of the wreath. Using 1- and ¾-inch punches, make several circles of each size. Cover the donut shape with the circles, using glue stick to secure. Raise some of the circles from the surface using dimensional adhesive dots. Use a ¼-inch paper punch to craft berries from red or dark pink cards, using adhesive dots to secure. Knot a short piece of ribbon for the bow and thread a ribbon hanger through a hole punched near the top.

Cute Boot

A few quick stitches and a couple dabs of hot glue and you have adorable paper boots to trim the tree. Tuck in a candy cane and these wondrous wears do double duty as treat holders.

1 **Trace the boot,** trim, and cuff patterns on page 155. Use the patterns to cut out 2 facing boot shapes, contrasting trim, and cuff pieces from scrapbook paper using straight- and decorative-edge scissors as shown.

2 **Machine-stitch the boot trim** to the corresponding boot piece as shown on pattern.

3 **Fold the cuff in half** as indicated on pattern. Align boot front and back; place cuff fold against top right edge. Stitch the layers together 1/8 inch from edge; leave top open.

4 **Hot-glue 2 buttons to cuff** and a rickrack loop to inside of upper right corner of stocking.

Pieced Pretties

■ Crafted using the same technique as for the spheres on pages 34–35, these trims resemble quilted bits of fabric. Join six folded circles as shown; adhere to white cardstock circle (see pattern page 154). Trim a narrow border with decorative-edge scissors and hot-glue a pom-pom in the center.

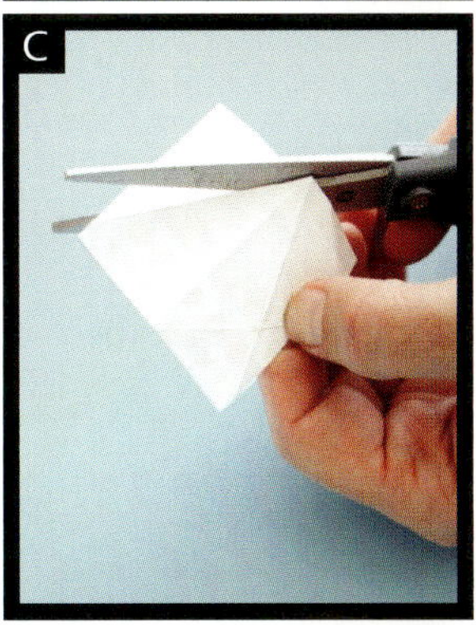

Tinsel-Town Stars

■ Underneath these pretty ornaments are cardboard stars eager to be dressed up for the season.

What You'll Need

- [ ] cardboard dimensional stars
- [ ] pencil
- [ ] holiday-theme scrapbook paper
- [ ] scissors
- [ ] glue stick
- [ ] hot-glue gun; glue sticks
- [ ] silver chenille stems

1 Trace around star onto the wrong side of scrapbook paper as shown in Photo A; cut out. Use glue stick to adhere paper to star back.

2 For each star point, cut a small square of scrapbook paper, large enough to cover point; fold in half vertically. Align fold with raised edge of star; fold paper edges along star edges and inside lines as shown in Photo B. Cut out diamond shape along folds as shown in Photo C.

3 Use glue stick to secure paper diamond shapes onto each star point as shown in Photo D.

4 Cut 5 chenille stem pieces to cover star form between paper pieces. Apply hot glue into crevice. Carefully place chenille stem piece onto glue as shown in Photo E. Continue adding chenille stem pieces, meeting at center point of star.

5 Hot-glue chenille stems around edge of star, piecing as needed.

Inspired by a Song

Blend the lyrics of your favorite Christmas carols into holiday decorating for fun touches that are worth singing about.

Name That Place

■ A small snippet from sheet music is all it takes to transform a plain paper place card into one that brings melody to the table.

Carol Claim

■ Metal-edge tags available in office supply and scrapbooking stores make perfect glass charms. Use a circle cutter to make circles from sheet music to fit tags; glue in place. Use a paper punch to make a hole at the top. Hot-glue chenille stem around the edge and a trio of jingle bells near the hole. Short lengths of ball chain attach the charms to glass stems. Organize glasses on record albums for a fun touch.

Words to Eat By

■ Be on the lookout for holiday music books at flea markets and thrift shops. Carefully remove the staples and you'll have instant place mats. To carry out the music theme, use 45s in coordinating colors as napkin rings.

Candle
Wraps

■ Add interest to candles
by surrounding them in
sleeves cut from music-
theme scrapbook paper.
To hide the seam, use
double-sided tape to
secure overlapping layers.
Remove the paper sleeves
before burning the
candles.

Musical Notes

■ Craft gift tags and thank-you cards using pieces of holiday sheet music layered on festive papers. Frame a music-theme charm for a snazzy focal point.

Music Men

■ Whether they're hanging on a tree or trimming a package, these little fellas send a merry message. Use pattern pieces on page 157 to cut pieces from sheet music and scrapbook papers. To outline body pieces, use circle cutters ¼ inch larger than the circles. To outline scarf and nose, glue cutout pieces to black and trim narrow borders. Glue pieces together as shown.

Jingle-Bell Bag

■ Create gift bags using laminated sheet music cut to desired sizes. Use a ruler and marking pen to mark holes ½ inch apart along edges; punch holes. Thread a darning needle with two plies of metallic thread; stitch pieces together. Punch a pair of holes on front, thread with chenille stem, and use it to secure a ribbon bow and jingle bells.

Knit Wits

From vintage mittens on the table to flea-market sweater cutouts trimming the mantel, these projects will have you on the search for pretty knits that fit right in with your wintry decor.

Cute Cuffs

■ Candles warm up any room in the winter, especially when decked in cozy knits. The cuddly wraps are simply sweater sleeves with the cut edges turned either up or under. When lighting the candles, be sure to snug down the knit accents.

Mitten Smitten

■ Surprise Santa with new shapes hanging from the mantel on Christmas Eve. These oversize mittens are sewn from secondhand sweaters and trimmed with an easy-to-do chain-stitch edging.

What You'll Need
☐ tracing paper
☐ pencil
☐ scissors
☐ tight-knit sweaters
☐ sewing machine
☐ thread; crochet hook
☐ yarn to contrast sweater
☐ darning needle
☐ 1-inch sparkly pom-pom trim to match yarn
☐ fiberfill (optional)

1 Enlarge and trace the mitten pattern on page 154. Use the pattern to cut front and back mitten pieces.

2 With right sides facing, machine-sew the mitten pieces together using a ¼-inch seam allowance. Turn right side out.

3 Cut four 5-yard-long pieces of yarn; knot ends together. Crochet a chain stitch using all 4 plies of yarn, making it long enough to go around curved edge of mitten. Thread darning needle with a single ply of yarn; sew chain-stitch trim to mitten edge, tucking ends of trim inside the mitten.

4 To make a rosette, cut off sweater sleeve 10 inches from cuff edge. Trim off sleeve seam so piece measures 10x4 inches. Fold piece lengthwise, raw edges together. With threaded darning needle, gather raw edges ½ inch from edge. Pull yarn tight to draw sweater piece into a circle; knot.

5 Wrap yarn around 3 fingers 20 times; slide off fingers. Thread a 10-inch length of yarn through the center of yarn bundle; tie tightly and knot. Trim yarn ends to make a 2½-inch pom-pom. Stitch sparkly pom-pom in the center.

6 Sew pom-poms to center of rosette; sew onto upper right corner of mitten. Sew a hanging loop behind rosette.

7 If mittens tend to flop when they are hanging, stuff them gently with a thin layer of fiberfill.

Rustic
Charm
Handknit mittens bring
a touch of warmth to
the table. For each place
setting, fill with silverware
and an artificial sprig of
greenery. Thread jumbo
yarn through the mitten's
knitted fabric and tie into
a generous bow as the
finishing touch.

Merry Muffler

■ Give a knit scarf the run of your holiday table. A scarf lends a soft touch and protects the tabletop.

Sock-Top Trims

■ When sock toes wear away, fashion tops into homespun trims. Use a pencil to poke holes in opposite sides of a plastic foam ball. Cut off sock 6 inches from top and pull over ball, open ends around indents. Use the pencil to push knit ends into indents. Pin a braided yarn hanger to top.

Mix and Match Pillow

■ Make a new throw pillow from old or thrift shop sweaters. For the base, cut front and back slightly larger than pillow size using bottom sweater edge as one pillow edge. With right sides facing, machine-stitch the nonfinished edges using $1/2$-inch seams. Turn right side out, insert pillow form, and slip-stitch opening closed. Cut a band from second sweater; sew a trio of buttons on the band. Turn under raw edges. Slip band around the pillow; tack in place.

Very Merry Mantels

Set the stage for St. Nick's visit with a snazzy mantelscape overlooking ready-to-fill stockings.

Festive Forest

■ Create a miniature wintry scene by combining tabletop trees and silver deer figurines atop the mantel. Center a larger item, such as a framed Christmas picture, for a cheery focal point. To make one of the trees stand out, hot-glue miniature ornaments to it.

Merry Ol' Souls

■ Whether you choose snowmen, Santas, elves, or other holiday friends, group a collection of holiday-time characters to get the party started. For a fun accent, prop a variety of sparkling snowflakes behind them.

All Aglow

■ The key to a cozy setting is to choose a simple color scheme and stick to it. Christmas red and snow white are accented with shiny silver for a tradition with a twist. Use a variety of shapes and styles of candles and candleholders because it's the color that unites the mantel arrangement.

Bring visions of St. Nick's icy magical homeland to your home this holiday season. Marry cool blue with Santa red for a wonderland of merry surprises. And no need to hunt for new table linens; a fresh roll of wrapping paper that fits the theme is all it takes.

North Pole Inspiration

Treasure Troves

■ With a little trimming, boxes make inexpensive favors. Wrap bottoms and lids separately and place a tiny bow on the lid. Fill the box with wrapped candies and add a tiny bottlebrush tree as an extra take-home trinket.

Dinner with Kris Kringle

■ A few vintage Santas anchor this fantasyland. Towering candleholders topped with round candles appear as snowballs while snowflakes, laid flat, add sparkle below.

Details, Details

■ Honor the man of the hour by labeling the glass bell with "jolly ol' elf." Use icy blue alphabet stickers for a subtle appearance.

Merry Milk

■ Give the kids a few surprises of their own. Fill a holiday-theme clear glass with milk and stir in a drop of blue food coloring. You'll have them convinced it came straight from Santa's North Pole kitchen.

He's Gonna Find Out

■ Toss some humor onto the table with naughty and nice ribbons tied onto ornaments sporting guests' names. These fun trims can be used as place cards, tied onto stems of glasses, or tucked into favor boxes.

Sweet Coaster

■ A large flat lollipop works wonders as a coaster. Leave on the wrapper and tie a ribbon bow around the stick as a final touch.

Rudolph Sighting

■ Trim an easy-sew felt stocking with an image of Santa's favorite sidekick. Accent his holly collar with sparkly pom-poms for added dimension.

- tracing paper
- pencil
- scissors
- felt in red, white, turquoise, and black
- shimmery-blue heavy thread
- sewing needle; thread
- straight pins
- small silver-flecked pom-poms in white, turquoise, and green
- large red pom-pom
- fabric glue
- ruler
- green rickrack
- sewing machine

1 **Trace the patterns on page 158**; cut out. Use patterns to cut 2 stocking pieces and the holly collar from red felt, the deer from white felt, and the eyelashes from black.

2 **Using blanket stitches** and blue thread, stitch deer shape to stocking front. Stitch holly in place and tack down small pom-poms. Sew on a large pom-pom for nose. Glue on eyelashes.

3 **Cut two 11×1½-inch strips** from turquoise felt. Using a needle and thread, gather one long edge of each piece to fit stocking top.

4 **Pin stocking front to back** around curved edges, sandwiching rickrack between layers. Pin gathered edge of 1 turquoise strip to inside of stocking front, again sandwiching rickrack between layers; repeat for back.

5 **Machine-stitch trims** to stocking top ⅛ inch from edge. Sew the curved edges together.

6 **Tack on a rickrack loop** as stocking hanger.

Elf Bites

■ Treat guests to an after-dinner sweet. Choose candies in red, white, and icy blue to carry out the color scheme.

Quick Grid

■ Once you've chosen your holiday color scheme, purchase a dozen 4-inch tiles to coordinate. Place them side by side to form a place mat. Place the tiles directly on a table covering or apply adhesive felt dots if you're setting the table without a cloth.

Tilings of Comfort & Joy

Polka-Dot Coasters

■ Dotted and delightful, these coasters protect the table during the holidays and all year long.

What You'll Need

- [ ] 6-inch color-backed clear glass tiles
- [ ] ten 1-inch adhesive dots
- [ ] etching cream
- [ ] paintbrush
- [ ] stiff felt
- [ ] hot-glue gun; glue sticks
- [ ] decorative-edge scissors
- [ ] chenille stems

1 Place an evenly spaced double row of 1-inch sticker dots along one edge of tile top as shown in Photo A.

2 Following the manufacturer's instructions, brush a coat of etching cream on tile top as shown in Photo B. Allow to set for the allotted time; rinse off cream with water.

3 Hot-glue the tile to felt; trim a narrow border.

4 Glue chenille stem around tile, piecing as necessary.

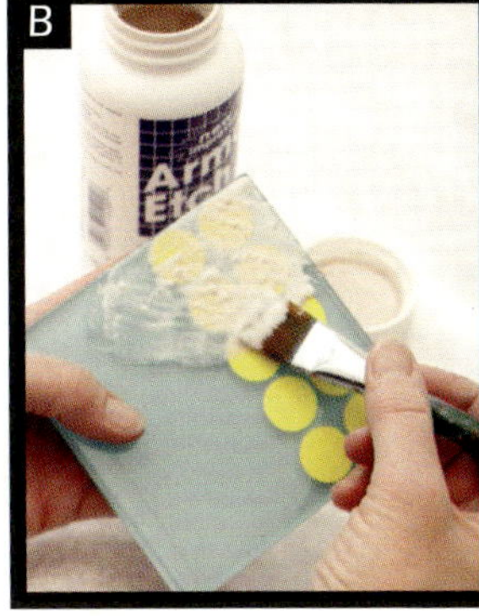

Package Pizzazz

■ Top holiday gifts with something special this year—the recipient's initials or a holiday word touted on tiny tiles. Wrap the gift, adding a layered band of ribbons. Hot-glue 1-inch tiles set on point to the ribbon. Press an alphabet sticker on each tile, framing each with chenille stem hot-glued around the edges.

Tiles with a Twist

■ Guests will feel extra special with these personalized markers twisted around their glass stems. Hot-glue a pair of 1-inch tiles on stiff felt; trim narrow borders. Press an initial sticker on each tile and edge with chenille stem as shown.

Decorated Diamonds

■ Two-inch tiles make clever ornaments for tabletop trees. Hot-glue a tile to stiff felt and trim a narrow border using decorative-edge scissors. With the tile on point, press a scrapbooking sticker in the center. Edge the sticker and tile with chenille stem and add a hanging loop.

Name Plates

■ Alphabet stickers make lettering name cards easy. And, if the guest list changes, you can make the switch quickly. Edge a long narrow tile by hot-gluing on a border of metallic chenille stem. If tile won't stand on its own, hot-glue a second tile behind the first.

Winter Sunshine

Luscious Layers

■ Start off the color scheme with yellow place mats topped with gold chargers and gold-edged plates. A golden paper doily adds to the elegance. To make poppers, wrap short cardboard tubes with coordinating tissue papers and a band of art paper, then tie the ends with ribbon.

Lemon and Shine

Brilliant yellow roses in a golden vase make a gorgeous centerpiece. Enhance the bouquet with gilded picks and the arrangement is unforgettable. Tie wide yellow satin ribbon around the vase and set it on matching paper. Surround the centerpiece with gold ornaments to complete the look.

Glass Glam

- Glittery adhesive scrolls from a scrapbooking store dress up goblets in seconds. Accent with a press-on gem or two and the glasses are ready for toasting. Accordian-folded napkins add to the formality.

Christmas Bells

- Glittered and golden, jingle bells look elegantly simple hanging from wide yellow satin ribbon. Be sure to knot the bow so it doesn't come loose from the weight of the bells.

Simply Stunning

- A large gold snowflake jingle bell is a subtle reminder of the season. To attach the sparkling bell, drill a pair of holes in a plastic or wood charger. Thread through a piece of yellow ribbon and tie on the bell. If the charger is glass or metal, use hot glue to attach the trim.

Gilded Branches

■ Carry out the gold and yellow theme with a tabletop tree touting the classy combination. Easy-to-make paper birds and beribboned ornaments stand out amidst gilded tree branches. Candy canes, in unexpected yellow, add a familiar Christmas shape.

Beribboned Beauty

■ Paint ornaments to coordinate with your lemony color theme. For each ornament, remove the topper and spray-paint the sphere; let dry. Hot-glue yellow satin ribbon flowers around the center. Replace the ornament topper.

Winged Wonder

■ Pretty papers in two simple shapes create this striking bird ornament. Use the pattern on page 155 to cut two facing body pieces and two facing wing pieces from yellow-and-gold paper. Adhere the wing shapes to two-sided metallic gold paper using glue stick and trim a narrow border with decorative scissors. Adhere one body shape to gold paper; trim a narrow border. Glue on the remaining body side. Using the pattern for positioning, attach the wings. Punch a small hole at the top of the bird body and attach a chenille stem hanger.

Following Yonder Star

We Three Kings

A trio of crowns represents the kings who followed the star to Bethlehem. These canvas versions shine with gold metallic paint and acrylic gems in rich vivid colors.

What You'll Need

- two 18-inch-square stretched canvases
- one 20-inch-square stretched canvas
- acrylic paint in black and metallic gold
- paintbrush
- tracing paper
- pencil
- scissors
- pencil with new eraser
- 2-inch dimensional cardboard stars with flat backs
- clear acrylic spray
- hot-glue gun; glue sticks
- acrylic gems in a variety of vivid colors

1 Paint each canvas black; let dry. Apply a second coat if needed; let dry.

2 Trace and enlarge the crown patterns on page 156; cut out. Trace around the rounded crown in the center of the large canvas and the remaining crowns on the small canvases.

3 Paint the crowns gold, allowing some of the black to show through the brushstrokes; let dry. Dip the pencil eraser in gold paint and dot evenly around each crown; let dry.

4 Paint the stars gold; let dry. Hot-glue a star to the top point of each crown.

5 In a well-ventilated work area, spray the paintings with clear acrylic; let dry.

6 Using the illustrations on page 156 for inspiration, hot-glue gem patterns onto the crowns. Glue a gem to the center of each star.

Glad Tidings

Spell out a Christmas message with glass alphabet ornaments gilded with gold, bronzed, and edged in black to give them an old-world look as shown on pages 70–71.

All Is Calm

As a wondrous reminder of the First Christmas, sculpt a nativity ornament from clay and whittle it to appear like wood.

What You'll Need

- white oven-bake clay, such as Sculpey
- waxed paper
- rolling pin
- tracing paper
- pencil
- scissors
- cutting board
- crafts knife
- paper clip
- wire cutters
- glass or metal baking pan
- gold acrylic paint
- paintbrush

1 Place a golf ball-size piece of clay between sheets of waxed paper. Use a rolling pin to flatten clay to ¼-inch thickness as shown in Photo A.

2 Draw an arched background pattern approximately 4 inches high by 3 inches wide onto tracing paper; cut out. Draw around the shape on the rolled-out clay. Slide a cutting board under clay; cut out the shape using a crafts knife as shown in Photo B.

3 Roll a long coil of clay to outline the arch of the background piece. Press onto the edge of the background piece. Roll three coils to form the roof and press onto background as shown.

4 Place a grape-size piece of clay on waxed paper; roll to approximately ⅛ inch thick. Use a crafts knife to cut out a star similar to the one shown. Press star to top of roof.

5 Use a wire cutter to snip off the end of a paper clip to use as a hanging loop. Press the open ends of the clip into the top of the roof under the star.

6 Using the photo, opposite, for placement and size relationships, shape and add clay pieces. Make small ropes for the hay, robe accents, and halo. Press pieces into place.

7 Bake the clay in the oven as directed by the manufacturer's instructions. Let cool.

8 Using a crafts knife, carve away tiny pieces from the clay ornament to resemble wood carving, as shown in Photo C.

9 Paint ornament gold; let dry.

Bearing Gifts

Small packages dressed in gold are reminiscent of those offered to baby Jesus. To blend with the colors of the crown, wrap the packages in gold metallic coordinating paper and accent with ribbons, folded paper, miniature ornaments, chenille stems, and jingle bells.

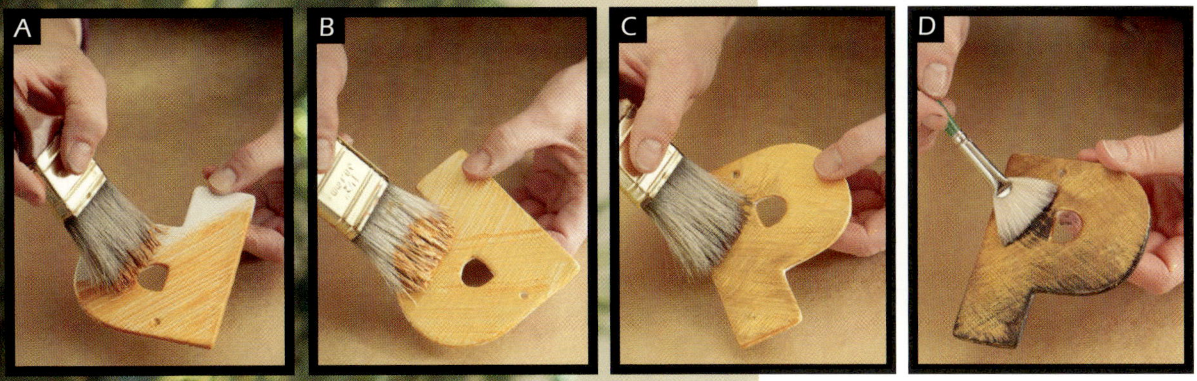

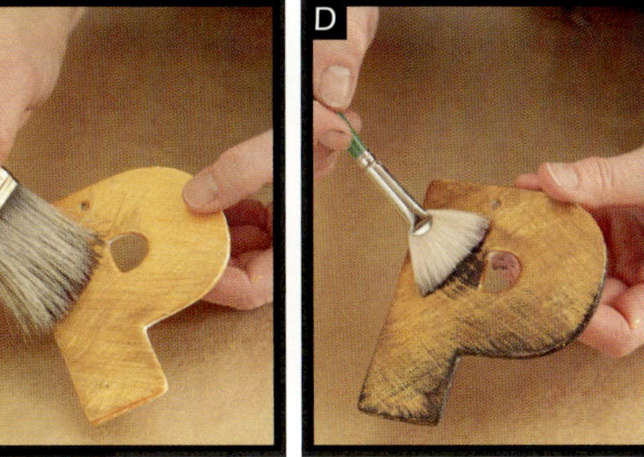

Garland of Peace

Bring a seasonal message to Christmas tree branches with garlands touting words of joy. Craft the letters in the same manner as for the stocking embellishments on page 67, then tie them together with heavy cord knotted at each letter top.

What You'll Need

- glass alphabet ornaments
- old bristle paintbrush
- acrylic paint in gold, bronze, and black
- fan-style paintbrush
- hot-glue gun; glue sticks
- acrylic gems
- heavy cord

1 For each letter use gold paint and brush strokes in one direction as shown in Photo A; let dry. Paint gold in the opposite direction as shown in Photo B; let dry.

2 With a little bronze paint on brush, paint Xs as in Photo C; let dry.

3 Using a fan-style paintbrush, very little black paint, and X strokes, brush the edges of the ornament to define the shape as shown in Photo D. Let paint dry.

4 Hot-glue 3 gems to the left side of each letter. Thread the hole with ribbon to hang.

Something Old

Blending vintage and brand-new pieces works like magic using a traditional holiday palette. Group large items in the center to create a focal point on which to build the tablescape.

Something New

Center of Attention

Scour flea markets and antiques stores for tins and boxes to draw interest to the center of the table. Tuck in fresh greenery to unite the interesting arrangement.

Sensational Server

■ A vintage wood box lined with feathery paper garland doubles as an instant serving piece for candy and cookies.

Sweet Ride

■ These adorable favors can be made by the dozens. Start with a pliable red plastic cup and trim off the rim with scissors. Round one side for the sleigh back and cut a dip for the front. Use low-temp glue to attach silver chenille stems around the edge. Glue a pair of candy cane runners to the bottom and this clever chariot is ready for goodies..

Place Setting with a Twist

■ Each guest's spot at the table looks special when you slip a holiday fabric napkin between the plates. Top off with an oversize candy stick tied with a generous length of red satin ribbon and you'll win the hostess with the mostest honor.

All Aglow

■ Illuminate the mat's motif by shaping it into a candle shade. Punch aligned holes along each short end of mat. Secure the ends together using metal brads. Place the shade over a glass hurricane with a candle nestled safely inside.

Pretty as a Place Mat

Special Delivery

■ Keep holiday cards handy in a holder crafted from a pair of matching plastic mats. Trim a small piece off the top of each and punch holes around the edges, aligning them on both mats. Stitch the front to the back using decorative cord and blanket stitches. Hang with a link chain.

1
2
3
4
5
6
7
8
9
10
11
12

The Twelve Days

Prolong the excitement that seems to build daily before Christmas with a calendar that makes the festivities last.

Cool Calendar

■ Plan an activity for each of the 12 days of Christmas, beginning with Christmas night and ending on Twelfth Night. Make a bulletin board marking the days and place a slip of paper with each day's activity in the corresponding paper pocket.

What You'll Need

- acrylic paint
- 18×14-inch bulletin board
- patterned paper
- crafts glue (optional)
- double-sided tape
- twelve 2¼×3½-inch red coin envelopes
- number stamps 0 through 9
- black ink pad
- 1¼-inch-diameter white sticker labels
- hot-glue gun; glue sticks
- 1¼-inch-diameter metal tag trims
- white paper

1 Paint the frame of the bulletin board and let dry. Apply patterned paper to the face of the board with crafts glue or double-sided tape.

2 Cut off the flap of each red coin envelope to leave the top open. Space the envelopes evenly on the bulletin board and attach with double-sided tape.

3 Stamp numbers 1–12 onto sticker labels and attach to envelopes. Apply hot glue to metal tag trims and attach to round stickers.

4 Write or print activities for each of the 12 days on slips of white paper. Insert the slips into the envelopes.

Creative Beginnings

Work of Art

■ Start off the new year right with a framed piece that elicits good wishes. Splatter-paint black cardstock with vivid colors and let it dry. Add a message with alphabet stickers to pop off the artistic background. Frame the piece with a wide white mat and a simple black frame. Show off the artwork on a black easel if desired.

Flecks and
Specks

■ Alternate black and white
napkins for added interest. To
splatter a border, open napkin
on a flat, protected work surface.
With a generous amount of fabric
or acrylic paint on a brush, flick
the paint onto the edges of the
napkin and allow to dry.

Initial Idea

■ Mark each guest's spot at the table with a large paintbrush touting his or her initials in alphabet stickers.

Portable Palette

■ Circular metal paint palettes, with their flat centers, make instant coasters. In lieu of paint in the wells, fill with nuts or other small snacks.

Quick Coaster

■ Back a quart-size paint can lid with felt and have a coaster that's in keeping with the party theme.

Color Crazy

■ Create unique tablecloths and runners using artist canvas or heavy cotton fabric by the roll. Splatter acrylic paint randomly or in patterns to create the desired look.

Paint Can Favors

■ New quart paint cans, available at paint stores, get a spiffy uplift wrapped with paint-splashed grosgrain ribbon. Line the can with a clear plastic bag and fill with snack mix or other surprises.

Choose a Color

■ Color swatch strips from paint stores enhance the painterly theme. Place them randomly on the table as conversation starters for guessing each other's favorite hues.

Festive Flourish ▶

Recycle burned-out bulbs as gift tags. Use a permanent marking pen to write a name on one bulb, then attach bulbs to a wrapped package using glue dots. Tuck in a sprig of artificial or fresh greenery to complete the accent.

In a Twinkling

Bright Lights

Glitter All Around

Crafts glue and glitter are all it takes to coat worn-out bulbs with a sparkling new coat. Present the trims in a clear glass bowl or tie together with cord to make a garland.

Ritzy Ring

Handcraft napkin rings that offer heartfelt season's greetings. Use hot glue to fasten green velvet and plaid ribbon ends together at the back. Tie narrow green satin ribbon around the metal part of the bulb. Another dab of hot glue attaches a sprig of greenery and an artificial holly berry to the knot of the bow.

Crafty Bow

Top a package with a Christmas-red bulb bow. Hot-glue bulbs in a circular pattern and top with a large snowflake jingle bell in the center.

▲ Jingle Bell Snowflake

Here's a bright little ornament even without electricity. On a flat surface hot-glue white Christmas lightbulbs in a symmetrical arrangement and let the glue set up. Glue a matching jingle bell in the center. To hang, wrap crafts wire around the threads on the top bulb.

SAVOR *the* SEASON

Cooking, sharing, and feasting! Whether you're hosting a special Thanksgiving or New Year's dinner or baking holiday treats to fill cookie trays and gift boxes, you'll find dozens of delicious ideas here.

Feast Potluck Style

Plan your Turkey Day festivities around a beautifully browned bird. For sides and dessert, invite guests to bring the crowd-pleasers featured here.

Traditional Roast Turkey
recipe on page 92

Cherry Cheesecake Kuchen
recipe on page 92

Traditional Roast Turkey

A medley of herbs gives this golden roasted bird fresh-from-the-garden flavor. Pictured on page 90.

    1 12- to 14-pound turkey
    1 tablespoon snipped fresh
         rosemary or 1 teaspoon dried
         rosemary, crushed
    1 tablespoon snipped fresh thyme
         or 1 teaspoon dried thyme,
         crushed
    1 tablespoon snipped fresh sage
         or 1 teaspoon dried sage,
         crushed
    1 teaspoon kosher salt or
         ½ teaspoon regular salt
    ½ teaspoon ground black pepper
    3 small onions, quartered
         (12 ounces total)
    3 medium carrots, peeled and cut
         into 2-inch chunks
    3 stalks celery, trimmed and cut
         into 2-inch chunks
    1 cup water
    1 tablespoon olive oil
         Fresh figs, halved tiny pears,
         thick apple slices, champagne
         grapes, and/or assorted fresh
         herbs (optional)

Preheat oven to 425°F. Remove neck and giblets from turkey, reserving neck bone. Rinse inside of turkey; pat dry with paper towels.

In a small bowl combine rosemary, thyme, sage, salt, and pepper. Season inside of body cavity with half of the herb mixture. Pull neck skin to the back; fasten with a skewer. Tuck the ends of the drumsticks under the band of skin across the tail. If there is no band of skin, tie the drumsticks securely to the tail with 100%-cotton kitchen string. Twist wing tips under the back.

Place turkey, breast side up, on a rack in a shallow roasting pan. Arrange onions, carrots, celery, and neck bone around turkey in roasting pan. Pour the water into the pan. Brush turkey with oil. Sprinkle turkey with remaining herb mixture. Insert an oven-going meat thermometer into the center of an inside thigh muscle; the thermometer should not touch bone.

Cover turkey loosely with foil. Roast for 30 minutes. Reduce oven temperature to 325°F. Roast for 2½ to 3 hours more or until the thermometer registers 180°F. About 45 minutes before end of roasting, remove foil and cut band of skin or string between drumsticks so thighs cook evenly. When turkey is done, juices should run clear and drumsticks should move easily in their sockets.

Remove turkey from oven. Transfer to a serving platter (reserve mixture in pan for gravy). Cover; let stand for 15 to 20 minutes before carving. If desired, garnish platter with figs, pears, apple slices, champagne grapes, and/or fresh herbs. Makes 24 (4-ounce) servings.

Cherry Cheesecake Kuchen

Cherry pie filling and a cream cheese mixture top a sweet, yeast-leavened dough for a dessert that's simply divine. Pictured on page 91.

    2¼ cups all-purpose flour
      1 package active dry yeast
      ½ cup milk
      ½ cup sugar
      ¼ cup butter
      ½ teaspoon salt
      2 eggs
      1 8-ounce package cream cheese,
           softened
      1 8-ounce carton dairy sour cream
      ¼ cup sugar
      1 tablespoon all-purpose flour
      ½ teaspoon vanilla
      1 egg, lightly beaten
      ½ teaspoon finely shredded
           lemon peel
      1 21-ounce can cherry pie filling
      ½ teaspoon almond extract
           Cherry pie filling (optional)
           White chocolate curls (optional)

Grease a 9-inch springform pan; set aside. Combine 1¼ cups of the flour and the yeast; set aside.

In a small saucepan heat and stir milk, ½ cup sugar, butter, and salt just until warm (120°F to 130°F) and butter almost melts. Add milk mixture and the 2 eggs to flour mixture.

Beat with an electric mixer on low to medium for 30 seconds, scraping sides of bowl constantly. Beat on high for 3 minutes. Beat in as much of the remaining 1 cup flour as you can with the mixer. Stir in any remaining flour.

Transfer dough to prepared pan; spread evenly (dough will be sticky). Cover and let rise in a warm place until double in size (about 1 hour).

Preheat oven to 350°F. In a mixing bowl combine cream cheese, sour cream, ¼ cup sugar, 1 tablespoon flour, and vanilla. Beat with electric mixer on medium until smooth. Stir in 1 egg and lemon peel; set aside.

In another bowl stir together pie filling and almond extract. Spoon cherry mixture over dough in pan. Spoon cream cheese mixture over cherry mixture, spreading evenly.

Bake about 45 minutes or until center appears set when gently shaken. Cool in pan on a wire rack for 30 minutes. Using a small sharp knife, loosen crust from sides of pan and cool for 1 hour.

Cover and chill at least 4 hours before serving. Remove sides of pan just before serving. If desired, spoon additional cherry pie filling on top and garnish with chopped white chocolate. Makes 12 to 16 servings.

Herbed Mushroom Stuffing
recipe on page 95

Broccoli-Cauliflower-Raisin Salad

Herbed Mushroom Stuffing

Cook this savory stuffing in a slow cooker and it totes easily to a holiday gathering. Toss in the toasted pecans just before serving to add flavor and crunch. Pictured on page 93.

- 4½ cups sliced fresh mushrooms (12 ounces)
- 1 cup sliced celery
- 1 cup chopped onion (1 medium)
- 6 tablespoons butter
- ⅓ cup snipped fresh basil and/or rosemary or 1 tablespoon dried basil and/or rosemary, crushed
- ½ teaspoon black pepper
- 12 cups dry whole wheat and/or sourdough bread cubes* (18 to 21 slices)
- 1 14-ounce can chicken broth
- ¾ cup pecan halves, toasted

In an extra-large skillet cook mushrooms, celery, and onion in hot butter over medium heat for 5 minutes. Remove from heat. Stir in basil and pepper.

In an extra-large bowl combine mushroom mixture and bread cubes. Drizzle with chicken broth to moisten, tossing lightly to combine. Transfer bread mixture to a 3½- or 4-quart slow cooker.

Cover and cook on low-heat setting (do not use high-heat setting) for 3½ to 4 hours. Just before serving, gently stir in pecans and, if desired, transfer to a serving dish. Makes 12 side-dish servings.

***NOTE:** To dry bread cubes, spread cubes in a 15½×10½×1-inch baking pan. Bake, uncovered, for 10 to 15 minutes or until cubes are dry, stirring twice. Cool. (Cubes will continue to dry and crisp as they cool.) Or let bread cubes stand, loosely covered, at room temperature for 8 to 12 hours.

Broccoli-Cauliflower-Raisin Salad

- 6 cups broccoli florets
- 3 cups cauliflower florets
- ½ cup golden raisins
- ⅓ cup walnut pieces, toasted
- ¼ cup olive oil or canola oil
- ¼ cup cider vinegar
- 1 teaspoon salt
- 1 teaspoon honey or sugar
- ½ teaspoon dried basil, crushed
- ½ teaspoon black pepper
- ¼ teaspoon crushed red pepper (optional)

In a saucepan bring 2 inches of water to boiling. Add broccoli, return to boiling. Cook, covered, for 2 minutes or until broccoli is crisp-tender and bright green; drain. Rinse with cold water; drain well.

In the same saucepan cook cauliflower in water using the same method as for broccoli.

In a 2- to 2½-quart bowl layer half the broccoli, cauliflower, raisins, and walnuts. Repeat layers. Cover and chill. Combine olive oil, vinegar, salt, honey, basil, black pepper, and red pepper. Add dressing just before serving and toss mixture to coat. Makes 10 servings.

Cranberry-Clementine Sauce

Take advantage of seasonal clementines, small, thin-skinned oranges with a red-orange flesh and tangy-sweet flavor.

- 4 clementines or 2 oranges
- 2 12-ounce packages fresh or frozen cranberries
- 1 cup sugar
- ½ cup water
- 1 teaspoon dried juniper berries (optional)
- 2 tablespoons fresh lemon juice

Cranberry-Clementine Sauce

Using a vegetable peeler, remove a 5×1-inch strip of peel from a clementine; place peel in a 4-quart saucepan. Trim ends of clementines. Standing each fruit on a cut end, trim peel and white pith away from sides with a sharp knife. Hold each fruit over a bowl to catch juice and cut segments free from membranes. Halve each segment crosswise; set clementines and juice aside.

Add cranberries, sugar, and the water to saucepan. If using juniper berries, place them in center of a double-thick, 6-inch square of 100%-cotton cheesecloth. Tie with clean kitchen string; add to saucepan. Bring to boiling; reduce heat. Simmer, uncovered, for 8 to 10 minutes or until cranberries burst and mixture is slightly thickened and bubbly, stirring occasionally.

Remove and discard bag of juniper berries. Transfer cranberry mixture to a bowl. Sir in lemon juice, reserved clementine segments, and 2 tablespoons of juice from the clementines. Cool slightly. Cover and chill.

TO MAKE AHEAD: Prepare sauce as directed. Cool; cover and chill for up to 3 days.

Crock-Roasted Root Vegetables

Savory Holiday Bread

This cheesy bread gets its festive colors from dried tomatoes and green onion tops. Rather than tossing the tasty white section of the green onions, substitute it for regular onions in other holiday recipes.

    3 cups all-purpose flour
    2 cups shredded Italian-style cheese
       blend (8 ounces)
    2 teaspoons baking powder
    1 teaspoon salt
    ½ teaspoon garlic powder
    3 eggs, beaten
    1 5-ounce can (⅔ cup) evaporated
       milk
    ⅓ cup thinly sliced green onion tops
    ¼ cup butter, melted
    ¼ cup oil-packed dried tomatoes,
       drained and finely chopped
    1 egg yolk
    1 tablespoon water

Preheat oven to 350°F. Grease a large baking sheet; set aside.

In a large bowl stir together flour, cheese, baking powder, salt, and garlic powder. Add eggs, milk, green onions, melted butter, and dried tomatoes. Stir until combined.

Turn dough out onto a lightly floured surface. Knead dough by folding and gently pressing it for 10 to 12 strokes or until dough holds together. Divide dough into 3 equal pieces. Roll each piece into a 14-inch rope. Place ropes 1 inch apart on the prepared baking sheet; braid ropes, pinching ends to seal.

In a small bowl beat together egg yolk and the water. Brush top of bread with egg yolk mixture.

Bake about 40 minutes or until golden brown. Transfer to a wire rack and cool completely. Makes 1 loaf (18 servings).

Crock-Roasted Root Vegetables

This hearty mixture of vegetables is seasoned with garlic, salt, and pepper and drizzled with olive oil. Best of all, the veggies cook unattended in a slow cooker.

    1 pound butternut squash, peeled
       and cut in 2-inch pieces
    8 ounces tiny new potatoes,
       halved
    8 ounces beets, peeled and cut
       into 1-inch pieces*
    8 ounces turnips or rutabagas,
       peeled and cut into 1-inch
       pieces
    1 cup packaged peeled fresh baby
       carrots
    1 small red onion, cut into ½-inch
       wedges
    8 cloves garlic, peeled
    2 tablespoons olive oil
    ½ teaspoon salt
    ½ teaspoon black pepper
       Chopped fresh parsley

In a very large bowl combine squash, potatoes, beets, turnips, carrots, onion, and garlic. Drizzle with olive oil and toss to coat. Sprinkle with salt and pepper. Place squash mixture in a 3½- or 4-quart slow cooker.

Cover and cook on high-heat setting for 3 to 4 hours or until vegetables are tender when pierced with a fork. Sprinkle with parsley. If desired, transfer vegetables to a serving dish. Makes about 12 side-dish servings.

***NOTE:** The deep red color of the beets bleeds out during cooking and tints the other vegetables red. If you like, omit the beets.

Savory Holiday Bread

Barley Soup
with Meatballs

Gather for Soup

Whether you plan a winter outing, Christmas caroling, or a tree-trimming party, end it on a simply delicious note with this warm and hearty selection.

Barley Soup with Meatballs

A trio of winter vegetables—squash, carrots, and parsnips—stars in this warming soup.

  4 slices bacon or peppered bacon
  ½ cup chopped onion (1 medium)
  2 cloves garlic, minced
  1 1- to 1½-pound butternut or
     acorn squash, peeled and cut
     into ¾-inch pieces (about
     4 cups)
  2 medium carrots, peeled and cut
     into ¾-inch pieces
  2 medium parsnips, peeled and
     cut into ¾-inch pieces
  4 14-ounce cans reduced-sodium
     chicken broth or lower-sodium
     beef broth (about 7 cups)
  1 cup apple juice or water
  1 teaspoon dried Italian seasoning,
     dried thyme, or dried
     oregano, crushed
  1 cup quick-cooking barley
 24 frozen cooked meatballs,
     thawed (about two-thirds of
     a 16-ounce package)
     Salt
     Black pepper

In a large pot cook bacon until crisp. Remove bacon from pot, reserving 1 tablespoon of the drippings in pot. Drain bacon on paper towels; set aside.

Cook onion and garlic in reserved drippings over medium heat until tender. Add squash, carrots, and parsnips; cook for 5 minutes more, stirring occasionally. Add broth, apple juice, and Italian seasoning. **Bring to boiling;** stir in barley. Reduce heat. Cover and simmer for 10 to 15 minutes or until barley and vegetables are tender. Add meatballs; heat through. Season to taste with salt and pepper.

Crumble cooked bacon and sprinkle over each serving.

TO MAKE AHEAD: Prepare as directed, except place cooked bacon in a resealable plastic bag. Quick-chill soup by placing pot in sink filled with ice water, stirring frequently. Transfer soup to an airtight container. Store soup and bacon in refrigerator up to 3 days. Reheat soup in a large pot over medium heat until heated through and sprinkle with bacon.

Garlic-Herb Challah
recipe on page 101

Turkey Tortilla Soup

Garlic-Herb Challah

Present the beautifully braided loaves in cloth-lined baskets Pictured on page 99.

- 1¾ cups warm water (105°F to 115°F)
- 2 tablespoons honey
- 2 packages active dry yeast
- 4 cloves garlic, minced
- 1 teaspoon dried basil, crushed
- 1 teaspoon dried rosemary crushed
- 1 teaspoon dried thyme, crushed
- 4 eggs, lightly beaten
- ½ cup olive oil
- 1 tablespoon salt
- 7½ to 8 cups bread flour or 8 to 8½ cups all-purpose flour
- 3 tablespoons butter, melted
- 1 teaspoon dried basil, crushed
- 1 teaspoon dried thyme, crushed
- 1 clove garlic, minced

In a large bowl combine the 1¾ cups warm water, the honey, and yeast. Stir in 4 cloves garlic and 1 teaspoon each of basil, rosemary, and thyme. Let stand 10 minutes or until yeast is dissolved and foamy. Using a wooden spoon, stir in eggs, olive oil, and salt. Gradually stir in as much of the flour as you can.

Turn dough out onto a lightly floured surface. Knead in enough of the remaining flour to make a moderately soft dough that is smooth and elastic (5 to 7 minutes total). Shape dough into a ball. Place in a lightly greased bowl, turning once to grease surface. Cover and let rise in a warm place until double in size (1 to 1½ hours).

Punch dough down. Turn out onto a lightly floured surface. Cover with a clean kitchen towel and let rest for 10 minutes.

To shape spiral loaves, divide dough into 3 portions. Divide each portion into thirds (9 portions total). Gently roll each portion into a 24-inch-long rope. Braid 3 ropes at a time to make 3 braids; shape each into a spiral loaf.

Cover and let rise in a warm place until nearly double in size (about 30 minutes).

Preheat oven to 350°F. In a small bowl combine the melted butter, 1 teaspoon each of basil and thyme, and 1 clove garlic, minced; brush over loaves. Bake for 30 to 35 minutes or until loaves sound hollow when lightly tapped. Immediately remove loaves from baking pans. Cool on wire racks. Makes 3 loaves (16 servings each).

Cashew-Apple Crunch Salad

Turkey Tortilla Soup

- 2 tablespoons vegetable oil
- 6 6-inch corn tortillas, cut into strips
- 4 14-ounce cans reduced-sodium chicken broth
- 2 cups purchased red or green salsa
- 4 cups cubed cooked turkey (1¼ pounds)
- 2 large zucchini, coarsely chopped
- Sour cream (optional)
- Lime wedges (optional)

In a large skillet heat oil over medium heat. Add corn tortilla strips, half at a time, and cook until crisp. Using a slotted spoon, remove the tortilla strips and drain on white paper towels.

In a large pot combine broth and salsa; bring to boiling over medium-high heat. Add turkey and zucchini; heat through. Serve in bowls topped with tortilla strips. If desired, top each serving with sour cream and add a squeeze of lime. Makes 8 servings.

Cashew-Apple Crunch Salad

- 2 10-ounce packages leafy romaine salad greens (8 to 9 cups)
- 2 medium Granny Smith apples, cored and thinly sliced
- ⅔ cup dried cranberries
- ⅔ cup dry-roasted cashews
- 2 medium shallots, thinly sliced
- 2 cloves garlic, minced
- ¼ cup olive oil
- 2 teaspoons honey
- 1 teaspoon Dijon mustard
- ¼ teaspoon salt
- ¼ teaspoon black pepper
- ¼ cup balsamic vinegar

In a large serving bowl toss together mixed greens, apples, cranberries, and cashews.

In a large skillet cook shallots and garlic in hot olive oil over medium heat for 3 minutes or until tender. Remove from heat. Whisk in honey, mustard, salt, and pepper until combined. Stir in vinegar. Add dressing to salad; toss to coat. Serve immediately. Makes 12 servings.

Mitten Cookies

*MITTEN STENCIL: Trace a mitten shape about 3 inches long on heavy cardboard or on the back of a stiff paper plate. Cut out mitten with a sharp knife.

Bean and Potato Chowder

Creamy and rich, this soul-satisfying soup—with its accompanying cheese toast—will be a hit at your soup supper.

- 2 20-ounce packages refrigerated diced potatoes with onions
- 2 14-ounce cans vegetable broth
- ⅔ cup all-purpose flour
- 2 cups shredded Swiss cheese (4 ounces)
- 6 cups milk
- 2 teaspoons dried Italian seasoning
- 2 15-ounce cans navy beans, rinsed and drained
  Salt and black pepper
  Bottled roasted sweet red pepper and chopped fresh parsley leaves (optional)
- 8 ½-inch slices Italian bread topped with shredded Swiss cheese, toasted (optional)

In a large pot combine potatoes and vegetable broth; cover and bring to a boil over high heat. Reduce heat. Simmer, covered, for 4 minutes.

In a large bowl toss together flour and 1 cup of the shredded cheese until cheese is coated. Gradually stir in milk until combined. Add milk mixture and Italian seasoning to potato mixture. Cook and stir over medium heat until thickened and bubbly. Stir in beans; cook and stir for 1 minute more. Season to taste with salt and pepper. If desired, top with sweet pepper and parsley and serve with cheese-topped bread. Makes 8 servings.

Mitten Cookies

- 1½ cups butter, softened
- 1⅔ cups granulated sugar
- 2 teaspoons baking powder
- ½ teaspoon salt
- 2 eggs
- ¼ cup buttermilk
- ½ teaspoon vanilla
- ⅓ cup ground toasted almonds
- 4 cups all-purpose flour
  Coarse colored sugars

In a large bowl beat butter with an electric mixer on medium to high for 30 seconds. Add granulated sugar, baking powder, and salt. Beat until combined, scraping sides of bowl occasionally. Beat in eggs, buttermilk, and vanilla until combined. Beat in ground almonds and as much of the flour as you can with mixer. Stir in any remaining flour. Cover and chill for 2 hours or until dough is easy to handle.

Preheat oven to 375°F. Using ⅓ cup dough for each cookie, shape dough into balls. Place on ungreased cookie sheet; cover with plastic wrap and flatten with your hand or bottom of a pie plate to 4- to 5-inch rounds, placing cookies 1½ inches apart.

Place a mitten cookie cutter or a stencil* over a cookie; sprinkle colored sugar inside the cutter or stencil. Remove and repeat with remaining cookies.

Bake about 14 minutes or until edges are firm and bottoms are browned. Cool on cookie sheet for 2 to 3 minutes. Transfer to wire rack and let cool. Makes 16 large cookies.

Bean and Potato Chowder

Sweets of the Season

Candies, fruits, and nuts make bars and cookies all dressed up and ready to impress.

Chewy Cherry-Almond Bars

Chewy Cherry-Almond Bars

For the best flavor, purchase real almond extract—not the imitation—for use in these decadent bar cookies.

1 cup butter, softened
2 cups packed brown sugar
2 teaspoons baking powder
1 egg
1 teaspoon almond extract
2 cups all-purpose flour
2 cups regular rolled oats
½ cup sliced almonds
1 12-ounce jar (1 cup) cherry preserves

Preheat oven to 350°F. Line a 13×9×2-inch baking pan with foil, extending foil over edges of pan. Grease foil; set pan aside.

In a large mixing bowl beat butter with an electric mixer on medium to high for 30 seconds. Add brown sugar and baking powder. Beat until combined, scraping sides of bowl occasionally. Beat in egg and almond extract until combined. Beat in as much of the flour as you can with the mixer. Using a wooden spoon, stir in any remaining flour, the oats, and almonds.

Remove ½ cup of the dough and set aside. Press the remaining dough evenly into bottom of the prepared baking pan. Spread with preserves. Crumble the reserved dough evenly over preserves layer.

Bake about 35 minutes or until lightly browned. Cool in pan on a wire rack. Using edges of foil, lift cookies out of pan. Cut into bars. Makes 36 bars.

TO STORE: Place in a single layer in an airtight container; cover. Store in the refrigerator for up to 3 days or freeze for up to 1 month.

Pumpkin-Spiced Star Cookies

Fudge Ecstasies

Pumpkin-Spiced Star Cookies

1 17.5-ounce package sugar cookie mix
⅓ cup butter, melted
1 egg
2 teaspoons pumpkin pie spice
½ teaspoon ground nutmeg
   Browned Butter Icing

Preheat oven to 375°F. In a large bowl combine dry cookie mix, melted butter, egg, pumpkin pie spice, and nutmeg. If necessary, gently knead until smooth.

On a lightly floured surface roll dough until ¼ inch thick. Using a 1½- or 2½-inch star-shape cookie cutter, cut out dough. Place 1 inch apart on an ungreased cookie sheet.

Bake about 8 minutes or until bottoms are light brown. Let stand for 1 minute on cookie sheet.

Transfer to a wire rack and let cool. Drizzle cookies with Browned Butter Icing. Makes 36 large stars or 72 small stars.

BROWNED BUTTER ICING: In saucepan cook and stir 2 tablespoons butter over medium-low heat about 15 minutes or until butter turns golden brown (watch closely so mixture doesn't scorch). Remove from heat. Stir in 2 cups powdered sugar, 2 tablespoons milk, and 1 teaspoon vanilla. Use immediately (icing will harden quickly).

Fudge Ecstasies

The dough will be thin and batterlike. Not to worry—it's actually the secret to these tender, rich chocolate delights.

1 12-ounce package (2 cups) semisweet chocolate pieces
2 ounces unsweetened chocolate, chopped
2 tablespoons butter
2 eggs
⅔ cup sugar
¼ cup all-purpose flour
1 teaspoon vanilla
¼ teaspoon baking powder
1 cup chopped cashews, pecans, or almonds

Preheat oven to 350°F. Grease a cookie sheet; set aside. In a heavy saucepan combine 1 cup of the chocolate pieces, the unsweetened chocolate, and butter. Cook and stir over low heat until melted. Remove from heat. Add eggs, sugar, flour, vanilla, and baking powder. Beat with a wooden spoon until combined. Stir in the remaining chocolate pieces and nuts.

Drop dough by rounded teaspoons 2 inches apart onto the prepared cookie sheet. Bake for 8 to 10 minutes or until edges are firm and surfaces are dull and crackled. Cool on cookie sheet for 2 minutes. Transfer cookies to a wire rack; cool. Makes about 36 cookies.

Cranberry-Eggnog Twirls

    1 cup butter, softened
 1½ cups sugar
    ½ teaspoon baking powder
    ½ teaspoon salt
    ½ teaspoon ground nutmeg
    2 eggs
    1 teaspoon rum extract
 3¼ cups all-purpose flour
    ½ cup cranberry preserves or jam
 1½ teaspoons cornstarch
    ½ cup finely chopped pecans,
        toasted*

In a large mixing bowl beat butter with an electric mixer on medium to high for 30 seconds. Add sugar, baking powder, salt, and nutmeg. Beat until combined, scraping side of bowl occasionally. Beat in eggs and rum extract until combined. Beat in as much of the flour as you can with the mixer. Using a wooden spoon, stir in any remaining flour. Divide dough in half. Cover and chill about 1 hour or until dough is easy to handle.

Meanwhile, for filling, in a small saucepan combine preserves and cornstarch. Cook and stir over medium heat until thickened and bubbly. Remove from heat. Stir in pecans. Set aside.

Between waxed paper roll half of the dough at a time into a 10-inch square. Spread with filling to within ½ inch of the edges; roll up dough. Moisten edges; pinch to seal. Wrap each roll in plastic wrap or waxed paper. Chill about 4 hours or until dough is firm enough to slice.

Preheat oven to 375°F. Line a large cookie sheet with parchment paper. Cut rolls into ¼-inch slices. Place 2 inches apart on the prepared cookie sheet.

Bake for 10 to 12 minutes or until edges are firm and bottoms are

Cranberry-Eggnog Twirls

light brown. Let stand for 1 minute on cookie sheet. Transfer to a wire rack and let cool. Makes about 60 cookies.

*NOTE: To toast nuts, preheat oven to 350°F. Spread nuts in a single layer in a shallow baking pan. Bake for 5 to 10 minutes or until nuts are slightly golden brown, stirring once or twice. Cool completely.

TO STORE: Layer cookies between waxed paper in an airtight container; cover. Store at room temperature for up to 3 days or freeze for up to 3 months.

Snickerdoodle Croissant Cookies

    ½ cup butter, softened
    2 3-ounce packages cream cheese,
        softened
    ½ cup packed brown sugar
    1 teaspoon vanilla
    ⅛ teaspoon salt
 1⅔ cups all-purpose flour
        Milk
    ½ cup finely chopped toasted
        pecans*
    2 tablespoons packed brown
        sugar
    ¾ teaspoon ground cinnamon
    ¼ teaspoon ground nutmeg
        Powdered sugar (optional)

In a large mixing bowl beat butter and cream cheese with an electric

mixer on medium for 30 seconds. Add ½ cup brown sugar, vanilla, and salt. Beat until combined, scraping sides of bowl occasionally. Beat in as much flour as you can with the mixer. Stir in any remaining flour.

Divide dough into 3 equal portions; shape each portion into a disk. Cover and chill dough for 1 hour.

Preheat oven to 350°F. Roll each portion of dough to a 9-inch round on a lightly floured surface. Lightly brush each round with milk. Combine nuts, 2 tablespoons brown sugar, cinnamon, and nutmeg. Sprinkle nut mixture evenly over dough, leaving a ½-inch border. Cut each circle into 12 wedges with a pizza cutter or sharp knife. Roll up each wedge, starting from the wide end. Bend ends of roll to shape it into a crescent. Place crescents 1 inch apart on ungreased cookie sheets.

Bake for 14 to 16 minutes or until bottoms are light brown. Cool cookies on cookie sheets on wire racks for 2 minutes. Transfer cookies to wire racks and cool completely. If desired, sprinkle with powdered sugar before serving. Makes about 36 cookies.

*NOTE: To toast nuts, preheat oven to 350°F. Spread nuts in a single layer in a shallow baking pan. Bake for 5 to 10 minutes or until nuts are slightly golden brown, stirring once or twice. Cool completely. Finely chop nuts and set aside.

TO STORE: Place cookies, without powdered sugar, in layers separated by pieces of waxed paper in an airtight container; cover. Store at room temperature for up to 3 days or freeze for up to 3 months. Thaw cookies if frozen. Sprinkle with powdered sugar before serving.

Snickerdoodle Croissant Cookies

Chocolate-Caramel
Thumbprints

Chocolate-Caramel Thumbprints

- 1 egg
- ½ cup butter, softened
- ⅔ cup sugar
- 2 tablespoons milk
- 1 teaspoon vanilla
- 1 cup all-purpose flour
- ⅓ cup unsweetened cocoa powder
- ¼ teaspoon salt
- 16 vanilla caramels, unwrapped
- 3 tablespoons whipping cream
- 1¼ cups finely chopped pecans
- ½ cup semisweet chocolate pieces
- 1 teaspoon shortening

Separate egg. Cover and chill egg white until needed. Set yolk aside.

In a large mixing bowl beat butter with an electric mixer on medium to high for 30 seconds. Add sugar and beat well. Beat in the egg yolk, milk, and vanilla until combined.

In a medium bowl stir together flour, cocoa powder, and salt. Add flour mixture to butter mixture; beat until well mixed. Cover and chill about 2 hours or until dough is easy to handle.

Preheat oven to 350°F. Lightly grease cookie sheets; set aside. In a small saucepan combine caramels and whipping cream; heat and stir over low heat until mixture is smooth. Set aside.

In a shallow dish beat egg white with a fork. Place pecans in another shallow dish. Shape dough into 1-inch balls. Roll balls in egg white; roll in nuts to coat. Place balls 1 inch apart on prepared cookie sheets. Using your thumb, make an indentation in center of each ball.

Bake about 10 minutes or until edges are firm. Spoon some of the melted caramel mixture into indentation of each cookie. (If necessary, reheat caramel mixture to keep it spoonable.) Transfer cookies to wire racks and let cool.

In another small saucepan combine chocolate pieces and shortening. Heat and stir over low heat until chocolate is melted and mixture is smooth. Let cool slightly.

Spoon chocolate mixture into a heavy resealable plastic bag; seal bag. Snip a small corner off bag. Drizzle chocolate mixture over cookies. Let stand until chocolate is set. Makes 36 cookies.

TO STORE: Place cookies in a single layer in an airtight container; cover. Store at room temperature for up to 3 days. Or freeze undrizzled cookies for up to 3 months. Thaw cookies; drizzle with chocolate and let stand.

White-Chocolate Cherry Shortbread

White-Chocolate Cherry Shortbread

- ½ cup maraschino cherries, drained and finely chopped
- 2½ cups all-purpose flour
- ½ cup sugar
- 1 cup cold butter
- 12 ounces white chocolate baking squares with cocoa butter, finely chopped
- ½ teaspoon almond extract
- 2 drops red food coloring (optional)
- 2 teaspoons shortening
  White nonpareils and/or red edible glitter (optional)

Preheat oven to 325°F. Spread marachino cherries on paper towels to drain well.

In a large bowl stir together flour and sugar. Using a pastry blender, cut in the butter until mixture resembles fine crumbs. Stir in drained cherries and 4 ounces (⅔ cup) of the chopped chocolate. Stir in almond extract and, if desired, food coloring. Knead mixture until it forms a smooth ball.

Shape dough into ¾-inch balls. Place balls 2 inches apart on an ungreased cookie sheet. Using the bottom of a drinking glass dipped in sugar, flatten balls to 1½-inch rounds.

Bake for 10 to 12 minutes or until centers are set. Cool for 1 minute on cookie sheet. Transfer cookies to a wire rack and let cool.

In a small saucepan combine remaining 8 ounces white chocolate and the shortening. Cook and stir over low heat until melted.

Dip half of each cookie into chocolate, allowing excess to drip off. If desired, roll dipped edge in nonpareils and/or edible glitter. Place cookies on waxed paper until chocolate is set. Makes about 60 cookies.

TO STORE: Layer cookies between waxed paper in an airtight container; cover. Store at room temperature for up to 3 days or freeze for up to 3 months.

Holiday Beef
Tenderloin

Ring in the New Year

This delectable sit-down dinner showcases the most tasteful sampling of holiday offerings that are sophisticated in style but not in preparation.

Crab-Topped Shrimp
recipe on page 114

Holiday Beef Tenderloin

1 medium onion, cut into 1-inch wedges
3 cloves garlic, peeled
2 tablespoons olive oil
2 14.5-ounce cans fire-roasted diced tomatoes, drained
½ teaspoon sugar
½ teaspoon kosher salt
½ teaspoon finely shredded orange peel

1 2½-pound center-cut beef tenderloin roast
1 tablespoon olive oil
1 teaspoon kosher salt
1 teaspoon freshly ground black pepper
Roasted small red onions, white onion wedges, garlic, and sprigs of fresh thyme and rosemary (optional)

Preheat oven to 425°F. For tomato jam, in a shallow baking pan combine onion and garlic. Drizzle with the 2 tablespoons oil; toss gently to coat. Spread in a single layer.

Roast, uncovered, for 15 minutes. Using a slotted spoon, remove garlic; set aside. Roast onion, uncovered, about 10 minutes more or until onion starts to brown. Cool slightly. Coarsely chop onion and garlic.

In a medium bowl stir together roasted onion and garlic, tomatoes, sugar, the ½ teaspoon salt, and orange peel. Set aside.

Meanwhile, trim fat from meat. Brush meat with the 1 tablespoon oil; sprinkle with the 1 teaspoon salt and the pepper. Place meat on a rack in a shallow roasting pan. If desired, insert an ovenproof meat thermometer into the center of the meat.

Roast, uncovered, for 35 to 40 minutes for medium-rare (135°F) or 45 to 50 minutes for medium (150°F). Remove tenderloin from oven. Cover with foil and let stand for 15 minutes before slicing. (The meat's temperature will rise 10°F during standing.) To serve, cut meat into ½-inch slices. Serve with tomato jam. If desired, garnish with red and white onions, garlic, and herb sprigs. Makes 8 servings.

TO MAKE AHEAD: Prepare tomato jam as directed. Transfer to an airtight container; cover. Store in the refrigerator for up to 3 days.

Green Beans with Lime

2 pounds fresh green beans
⅓ cup fresh Italian parsley
1 tablespoon snipped fresh
    rosemary
2 teaspoons finely shredded
    lime peel
1 tablespoon fresh lime juice
1 clove garlic, minced
2 tablespoons olive oil
⅓ cup hazelnuts, toasted*
    and chopped

Remove ends and strings from beans. Leave beans whole or cut into 1-inch pieces.

In a medium covered saucepan cook beans, covered, in a small amount of boiling salted water for 3 to 4 minutes or until crisp-tender; drain. Immediately plunge beans in ice water; let sit for 3 minutes or until cool. Drain well; set aside.

In a small bowl combine parsley, rosemary, lime peel, lime juice, and garlic; set aside.

In a large skillet heat olive oil over medium-high heat. Add beans. Cook, stirring occasionally, for 3 to 4 minutes or until heated through. If desired, season with salt and pepper. Remove from heat. Stir in lime mixture and hazelnuts. Makes 8 servings.

***NOTE:** To toast hazelnuts, place nuts in a single layer in a shallow baking pan. Bake in a 350°F oven for 5 to 10 minutes or until light golden brown, watching carefully to avoid burning and stirring once or twice. To remove the papery skins from hazelnuts, rub the nuts with a clean dish towel.

Petite Pesto-Parmesan Potatoes

20 tiny new potatoes (about
    2¼ pounds)
 4 ounces pancetta, chopped
⅔ cup light sour cream
 2 teaspoons snipped fresh chives
¼ teaspoon salt
¼ teaspoon cracked black pepper
½ cup refrigerated basil pesto
¼ cup shredded Parmesan cheese
    (1 ounce)
    Snipped fresh chives (optional)

Preheat oven to 425°F. Scrub potatoes with a vegetable brush; pat dry with paper towels. Prick potatoes with a fork. Arrange potatoes in a 15×10×1-inch baking pan. Bake for 20 to 30 minutes or until tender, stirring once.

Meanwhile, in a small skillet cook pancetta over medium heat until crisp. Drain pancetta on paper towels, discarding drippings. When potatoes are cool enough to handle, cut potatoes in half lengthwise. If necessary, cut a thin slice from each bottom to keep potato upright. Using a measuring teaspoon, scoop pulp out of each potato half, leaving a ¼-inch-thick shell. Place pulp in a medium mixing bowl.

Beat the pulp with an electric mixer on low. Add sour cream, the 2 teaspoons chives, the salt, and ¼ teaspoon pepper; beat mixture until smooth.

Spoon pesto into potato shells. Top with the mashed potato mixture. Place potato shells in a 3-quart rectangular baking dish. Sprinkle with pancetta.

Bake about 5 minutes or until heated through. Sprinkle with cheese. Bake about 2 minutes more or until cheese is melted. If desired, garnish with additional chives. Makes 10 servings.

*Petite Pesto-
Parmesan Potatoes*

Limoncello Cosmos

salad mixture. Toss lightly to coat. If desired, garnish with a few fresh raspberries. Makes 6 servings.

Crab-Topped Shrimp

It's a double seafood delight when a creamy mixture of lump crabmeat becomes the centerpiece of butterflied shrimp. Pictured on page 111.

16 fresh or frozen large shrimp in shells (about 12 ounces)
 1 ounce (2 tablespoons) cream cheese, softened
 2 tablespoons mayonnaise
 1 teaspoon Dijon mustard
 ⅛ teaspoon salt
 1 6.5-ounce can lump crabmeat, drained and flaked
 2 tablespoons finely chopped green onion
 2 tablespoons finely chopped roasted red sweet pepper
    Sliced green onion (optional)

Thaw shrimp, if frozen. Peel and devein shrimp, leaving tails intact. Rinse shrimp; pat dry with paper towels. Preheat oven to 425°F. Line a 15×10×1-inch baking pan with foil; set aside.

In a medium mixing bowl beat cream cheese with an electric mixer on medium until smooth. Beat in mayonnaise, mustard, and salt. Stir in crabmeat, green onion, and roasted red pepper until combined.

Butterfly shrimp by cutting through the rounded side almost to the other side. Open shrimp and lay flat, cut sides down, in prepared baking pan. Divide crab mixture among shrimp, shaping the mixture into a mound.

Bake about 10 minutes or until shrimp are opaque. If desired, sprinkle with additional sliced green onion. Serve warm. Makes 16 appetizers.

Limoncello Cosmos

   Ice cubes
 6 tablespoons vodka
 2 tablespoons Limoncello, chilled
 2 tablespoons cranberry juice
    Fresh cranberries
    Lemon peel twists

Fill a cocktail shaker three-fourths full of ice. Add vodka, Limoncello, and cranberry juice.

Cover and shake until the outside of the shaker becomes frosty. Strain into chilled martini glasses or other small glasses. Garnish with fresh cranberries and lemon peel strips. Makes 2 (2½-ounce servings).

Star Fruit Salad with Raspberry Vinaigrette

 3 tablespoons raspberry vinegar
 2 tablespoons salad oil
 1 tablespoon honey
 1 10-ounce package torn mixed Italian-blend salad greens
 1 medium star fruit (carambola), thinly sliced
 ½ small red onion, thinly sliced
    Fresh raspberries (optional)

In a screw-top jar combine vinegar, oil, and honey. Cover and shake well. In a large bowl toss salad greens with star fruit and onion. Shake dressing well and pour over

Star Fruit Salad with Raspberry Vinaigrette

Poached Pear Tart
with Shortbread Crust

2 small Bosc pears
1 cup apple juice
⅔ cup water
⅓ cup granulated sugar
1 vanilla bean, halved lengthwise
1 ½-inch piece peeled fresh ginger, cut into strips
1 ½ cups all-purpose flour
⅓ cup powdered sugar
⅔ cup cold butter, cut into 1-inch slices
½ cup granulated sugar
2 tablespoons cornstarch
2 cups milk
2 eggs, lightly beaten
4 teaspoons finely chopped crystallized ginger
1 ½ teaspoons cornstarch

Peel pears, leaving stems intact. Cut pears in half lengthwise. Remove cores from pears.

In a small saucepan combine apple juice, the water, the ⅓ cup granulated sugar, half of the vanilla bean, and the fresh ginger. Bring to boiling, stirring to dissolve sugar. Add the pear halves. Return liquid to simmering. Simmer, covered, for 15 to 20 minutes or until pears are just tender. Remove from heat and transfer the pears and poaching liquid to a bowl; cover and chill for at least 2 hours or up to 24 hours.

Preheat oven to 350°F. For crust, in a food processor,* combine flour and powdered sugar. Cover and process until combined. Add butter. Cover and pulse with on/off turns until mixture forms fine crumbs. Dough will look dry. Press mixture onto the bottom and 1½ inches up the side of a 9-inch springform pan. Line the crust with a double thickness of foil. Bake 12 minutes. Carefully remove foil. Bake 8 to 12 minutes more or until edges are lightly browned and bottom looks dry. Cool on a wire rack.

For custard, in a heavy medium saucepan combine the ½ cup granulated sugar and the 2 tablespoons cornstarch. Stir in milk all at once. Cook and stir over medium heat until mixture is thickened and bubbly. Cook and stir for 2 minutes more. Remove from heat. Gradually stir about 1 cup of the hot mixture into beaten eggs. Return all of the egg mixture to the saucepan. Stir in the crystallized ginger. Cook and stir until bubbly. Reduce heat. Cook and stir for 2 minutes more. Remove from heat. Place saucepan in a large bowl of ice water. Stir the custard for 2 minutes to cool quickly.

Using a small knife, scrape seeds from the inside of the remaining half of the vanilla bean; add to custard mixture. Pour custard into baked crust, spreading evenly. Cover and chill at least 4 hours up to 24 hours.

Remove pears from poaching liquid; set aside. For glaze, transfer ½ cup of the poaching liquid to a small saucepan. Discard remaining poaching liquid. Add 1½ teaspoons cornstarch to the saucepan. Cook and stir over medium heat until thickened and bubbly. Cook and stir 2 minutes more. Transfer to a small bowl; cover and cool to room temperature.

To assemble tart, slice pear halves to but not through the top to form fans. Arrange pear fans in center of tart to form a circle, placing the stem ends in the center of the tart. Drizzle cooled glaze evenly over top. Using a sharp thin knife, loosen side of crust from the pan. Remove side of pan before serving. Makes 10 servings.

*NOTE: If you do not own a food processor, combine flour and powdered sugar in a medium bowl. Using a pastry blender, cut in butter until mixture starts to cling together. Pat mixture into pan and continue as directed.

Follow these easy steps for prepping the pears. Simply cut each pear into ¾-inch slices, cutting to but not through the top of the pear. (A). Carefully spread out the pear slices to form a fan (B). Gently place fanned pears on tart with stem ends touching in the center of the tart (C).

Poached Pear Tart with
Shortbread Crust

Frost cupcakes with your favorite white frosting. For the stars, melt vanilla confectioner's coating according to package directions. Place in a resealable plastic bag. Snip a small hole in corner of bag. Pipe stars onto a waxed paper-lined cookie sheet. Chill in refrigerator until set. Brush stars with gold luster dust and insert in frosting. Sprinkle additional gold luster dust and white edible glitter over top.

In a Twinkling
Creative Cupcakes

Prepare your favorite white frosting. Place some of the frosting in a pastry bag with a writing tip. Microwave remaining frosting on high for 5 seconds or until it just starts to melt. Tint with blue food coloring. Dip tops of cupcakes into frosting; shake off excess frosting. Let dry at room temperature until set. Pipe on snowflake design and decorate with small white candies. Sprinkle granulated sugar over top.

Peppermint Twist

For peppermint frosting (enough to fill 12 cupcakes), beat ½ cup softened butter, one 7-ounce jar marshmallow creme, and 1 teaspoon peppermint extract until smooth. Gradually beat in 2 cups powdered sugar and 2 tablespoons milk. Beat in 3 cups powdered sugar. Fill each cupcake with 1 tablespoon frosting. Roll sides of cupcakes in crushed peppermint candies. Pipe remaining frosting on top and decorate with additional candies.

▲ Rudolph with the Shiny Nose

Sprinkle red and green nonpareils on frosted cupcake. Insert two mini pretzels into the frosting for antlers, a peanut butter cookie for the head, and miniature marshmallow halves for eyes. Use frosting to attach miniature semisweet chocolate pieces for the eyes and a red candy-coated chocolate piece for the nose.

Frosty's Back

Dip 2 marshmallows (1 regular size and 1 trimmed ¼ inch) into melted vanilla confectioner's coating and roll in flaked coconut for the body and head. Chill until set. For the hat brim, trim ¼ inch off another marshmallow. Form a rectangle out of remaining piece; dip both pieces into melted chocolate confectioner's coating and piece together to form hat. Chill until set. Build snowman, using melted confectioner's coating to secure the coconut-covered marshmallows and marshmallow hat. Attach miniature chocolate chips for eyes and small red candies for nose and buttons. Insert chow mein noodles for arms. Frost cupcake with your favorite white frosting. Sprinkle with coconut. Make a sled from 3 small candy canes. Place snowman on top and add a scarf made from a red fruit roll-up.

GIVE *from* the HEART

Nothing warms the heart during the holiday season like true gestures of thoughtfulness. These gift ideas are sure to convey that sentiment.

Gifts to Go

■ Be prepared for seasonal parties with a stash of wrapped hostess gifts. Wrap bottles with a sleeve of paper, folding top edge under about 3 inches. Cut slits into the folded edge to create a frilled collar. Tie with ribbon if desired. Cut fold-over tags from decorative cardstock, cutting a circle from one side to slip over the neck of the bottle.

Surprises by the Sleighful

When you have several people to remember at holiday time, these clever concoctions can be fashioned assembly-line style.

Common Scents

Homemade sachets make easy, affordable gifts you can create in bulk. Dress up easy-sew or purchased drawstring muslin bags with a pretty rubber-stamped design, then fill with fragrant cedar shavings. To get a two-tone design, ink the stamp and wipe off the areas where the second color is desired. Brush the second ink color onto the wiped-off portions and press onto the bag.

Let There Be Light

Share the gift of candlelight with gorgeous hurricanes that are as merry as the season itself.

Hurricane Season

■ To give glass a tree tattoo, wrap it in adhesive shelf paper. Draw simple tree designs on the paper and cut around them using a crafts knife. Peel off the tree designs. Etch the glass following the manufacturer's directions for etching cream. Rinse off the etching cream and remove the remaining adhesive paper.

Blooming Presentation

■ Red carnations, silver trays, and candles create dramatic centerpieces. To make them, cover moistened 12-inch floral-foam wreath bases with flowers. Hot-glue a white bead to the center of each carnation. Add a glass hurricane lamp with a white candle in the center of each ring.

Surprise Visitor

■ Have fun by giving the gift of St. Nick this Christmas. Pick up a vintage card featuring the jolly ol' soul at a flea market or antiques store. Back it with cardstock and frame the image in a berry-red frame.

Magical Mixes

From cookies and breads to snacks and seasonings, beautifully packaged mixes make the perfect gifts from your kitchen to those you love.

Toffee Blondies In a Jar

- 1 cup packed brown sugar
- ½ cup miniature semisweet chocolate pieces
- 1 cup all-purpose flour
- 1 teaspoon baking powder
- ¼ teaspoon salt
- ¾ cup coarsely chopped pecans or walnuts
- ½ cup toffee pieces or butterscotch-flavor pieces
- ¼ cup butter, melted and cooled
- 2 eggs, slightly beaten
- 1 teaspoon vanilla

Layer in a 1-quart glass jar or canister the following ingredients: brown sugar, chocolate pieces, flour, baking powder, salt, pecans, and toffee pieces. Tap jar gently on the counter to settle each layer before adding the next. Cover jar.

Store at room temperature for up to 1 month. Or attach baking directions and give as a gift.

To make blondies: Preheat oven to 350°F. Grease an 8×8×2-inch baking pan. In a large bowl combine butter, eggs, and vanilla. Stir in jar contents. Spread into prepared pan. Bake for 25 to 30 minutes or until set and golden brown and edges just begin to pull away from pan. Cool in pan on a wire rack. Cut into bars. Makes 16 brownies.

Coconut Crunch Cookie Mix

- ½ cup granulated sugar
- ½ cup chopped pecans or hazelnuts
- 1¼ cups flaked coconut
- 1 cup crushed cornflakes
- ¾ cup packed brown sugar
- ½ cup quick-cooking rolled oats
- 1¼ cups all-purpose flour
- 1 teaspoon baking soda
- 1 teaspoon baking powder
- ¼ teaspoon salt

Layer in a 1-quart container the following ingredients: granulated sugar, pecans, coconut, crushed cornflakes, brown sugar, and rolled oats. (Firmly pack each layer before adding the next.) Combine flour, baking soda, baking powder, and salt. Add flour mixture to container. Seal and store container in a cool, dry place for up to 1 month.

To make cookies: Preheat oven to 350°F. In a large mixing bowl mix contents of container until well blended. Add ½ cup softened butter, 1 lightly beaten egg, and 1 teaspoon vanilla. Mix until well combined. Shape dough into 1-inch balls. Place balls 2 inches apart on ungreased cookie sheet. Bake 10 to 12 minutes or until edges are light brown. Cool for 2 minutes on cookie sheet. Transfer cookies to a wire rack and let cool completely. Makes about 3 dozen cookies.

Coconut Crunch Cookies

Dress It Up

■ A fun bow festively adorns a fluted serving dish. Simply hot-glue a generous ribbon bow to the serving piece and glue a large jingle bell in the center.

Dress It Up

■ Line a decorative pail with a clear cellophane bag and fill it with mix. Tie the bag closed using wide decorative ribbon. Wire on a berried pick and a small ball ornament for the crowning glory.

Winter Trail Mix

    Orange-Pecan Crunch
  2 cups dried apricots
  1½ cups sesame sticks or sesame oat
      bran sticks
  1 5-ounce package yogurt-covered
      raisins
  1 cup whole hazelnuts

In a large bowl toss together
Orange-Pecan Crunch, apricots,
sesame sticks, yogurt-covered raisins,
and hazelnuts. Divide mixture
among 7 gift bags. Seal and store at
room temperature for up to 1 week.

Orange-Pecan Crunch: Line a
baking sheet with foil. Butter foil;
set aside. Combine ½ cup sugar
and 2 tablespoons butter in a heavy
skillet. Cook over medium-high heat,
shaking skillet occasionally; do not
stir. When sugar melts, reduce heat
to low. Cook, stirring frequently,
until sugar is golden brown. Stir in
1½ cups pecan halves, 1½ teaspoons
finely shredded orange peel, and
½ teaspoon vanilla. Spread onto
prepared baking sheet. Cool; break
into pieces. Store, covered, in a cool,
dry place for up to 1 week.

Mocha Hot Cocoa Mix

  3 cups nonfat dry milk powder
  1½ cups sifted powdered sugar
  1½ cups unsweetened cocoa
      powder
  ⅔ cup instant coffee crystals
  1 cup miniature semisweet
      chocolate pieces

Stir together milk powder,
powdered sugar, cocoa powder,
coffee crystals, and 1 teaspoon salt;
divide among 5 gift bags. Sprinkle
chocolate pieces into each bag. Seal
and store at room temperature up to
3 months. Makes 5 (3-serving) bags.

Mocha Hot Cocoa Mix

Trio of Dip Mixes

To make cocoa: Before using, stir
chocolate pieces into cocoa mix. For
each serving: Place ⅓ cup of mix in a
mug. Add 1 cup boiling water, stirring
until chocolate pieces melt. If desired,
top cocoa with marshmallows or
whipped cream.

Trio of Dip Mixes

Bloody Mary Dip Mix: Combine
⅔ cup (½ ounce) dried tomato slices*
or ⅓ cup chopped dried tomatoes,
2 teaspoons dried celery flakes,
1 teaspoon lemon-pepper seasoning,
and ¼ teaspoon sea salt in container.

Mediterranean Dip Mix:
Combine 1 tablespoon dried oregano,
crushed; ½ teaspoon ground cumin;
¼ teaspoon dried lemon peel; and
¼ teaspoon sea salt in a container.

Pesto Dip Mix: Combine ¼ cup
toasted pine nuts, 1 tablespoon dried
basil, ½ teaspoon garlic powder, and
¼ teaspoon sea salt in a container.

***NOTE:** Include instructions to
chop tomatoes before making dip.

To make dip, combine one 8-ounce
carton sour cream and contents of
one of the dip mixes. If preparing
Bloody Mary Dip, cover and chill dip
for 4 to 24 hours before serving.

Dress It Up

■ Nestle the bag of
mix in a cup or mug
for two gifts in one.
Seal and tie the bag
with festive red-and-
white stripe string.

Dress It Up

■ A small stack of
jars and/or tins makes
a pretty presentation.
Use glue dots to
prevent shifting and
tie a ribbon around
the stack. Write
directions on a piece
of white ribbon and
slip it under the bow.

Dress It Up

■ A tree-shape window cut into a gift bag takes on a seasonal spin. Back the cutout with clear cellophane taped to the inside. Glue on bright buttons as shown to accentate the design.

Tortellini-Vegetable Soup Mix

To celebrate the season, stock your friends' pantries with gift bags of minestrone-style mix. If you like, present a stirring spoon or soup ladle with each bag.

- 6 tablespoons instant chicken bouillon granules
- 2 tablespoons dried minced onion
- 1 tablespoon dried Italian seasoning, crushed
- 1 teaspoon black pepper
- ½ teaspoon garlic powder
- 3 bay leaves
- 2 6- to 8-ounce packages dried cheese-filled tortellini
- 2 4-ounce containers dried carrots, corn, peas, sweet peppers, and tomatoes*
- 4 cups dried tomato slices or dried tomato bits*

For seasoning mix, combine bouillon granules, dried onion, Italian seasoning, pepper, and garlic powder. Divide bouillon mixture and bay leaves among 3 small plastic bags. Seal bags and set aside.

Divide tortellini among 3 gift bags or 1-quart jars or containers. Divide dried mixed vegetables and dried tomato slices or bits among bags or jars. Place a bag of the seasoning mix in each bag or jar. Seal; store in a cool, dry place up to 3 months. Makes 3 gift bags or jars (4 main-dish servings per bag or jar).

To make soup: In a large saucepan bring 6 cups water to boiling. Add soup mix from bag or jar. Return to boiling; reduce heat. Cover and simmer about 15 minutes or until tortellini and vegetables are tender. Discard bay leaf.

***NOTE:** Look for dried vegetables displayed in the produce section of your supermarket.

Dress It Up

■ Put your computer skills to work to craft a sticker label for the rub jar using the sample, left, as a guide. Cut a white paper strip to fit around the jar and punch it with circles and snowflake shapes. Use the sticker label to hide the band ends and hold it in place around the jar.

Multipurpose Meat Rub

- 3 tablespoons dried basil
- 2 tablespoons dried oregano
- 1 tablespoon dried thyme
- 1 tablespoon kosher salt
- 1 teaspoon black pepper
- 1 teaspoon garlic powder
- 1 teaspoon onion powder

Combine all ingredients. Pour mixture into a small jar. Cover; store in a cool, dry place for up to 3 months. Stir or shake before using. Makes ½ cup mix.

To use as a rub: Brush desired cut of beef, pork, or poultry with olive oil. Crush some of the rub mixture and sprinkle evenly over meat; rub mixture into meat or poultry with your fingers. Grill or broil meat or poultry as desired. If desired, garnish with fresh herb sprigs.

To make Meat Marinade:
Combine 3 tablespoons olive oil, 3 tablespoons red wine vinegar, 2 teaspoons of dry Multipurpose Meat Rub, and 1 teaspoon Dijon mustard. Place 1 pound pork chops or tender beef steaks (such as ribeye, top loin, or sirloin) in a resealable plastic bag set in a shallow dish. Pour marinade over meat. Seal bag. Marinate in refrigerator 4 to 6 hours, turning bag occasionally. Drain meat; discard marinade. Grill or broil meat as desired.

Anise-Orange Bread Mix

- 2½ cups bread flour
- 1¼ teaspoons active dry yeast or bread machine yeast
- 2 tablespoons packed brown sugar
- 1½ teaspoons dried orange peel
- ¾ teaspoon anise seeds
- ¾ cup whole wheat flour
- ¼ cup chopped pecans
- ⅓ cup golden raisins
- ⅓ cup dark raisins
- 1 teaspoon salt

Layer in a 1-quart jar the following ingredients: half of the bread flour, the yeast, brown sugar, dried orange peel, anise seeds, whole

Dress It Up

■ Layers of ribbon transform a plain jar into something special. Use double-sided tape to hold the ribbon layers in place. For the finishing touch, print and cut a tag about the mix and tie it and a ribbon bow around the jar.

wheat flour, pecans, raisins, the remaining bread flour, and salt. Seal and store in a cool, dry place for up to 1 month. Makes enough mix for a 1½-pound loaf (12 slices).

To make bread: In a large bowl combine 1 teaspoon yeast and the bread mix from the jar. Set aside. In a small saucepan heat and stir ¾ cup milk, ¼ cup water, and 3 tablespoons butter just until warm (120°F to 130°F) and butter almost melts. Add milk mixture and 1 egg to bread mix in bowl. Stir with a wooden spoon until combined.

Turn out dough onto a lightly floured surface. Knead in 2 to 6 tablespoons all-purpose flour to make a moderately stiff dough that is smooth and elastic (6 to 8 minutes total). Shape dough into a ball. Place in a lightly greased bowl, turning once to grease the surface of the dough. Cover; let rise in a warm place until double in size (45 to 60 minutes).

Punch dough down. Turn out dough onto a lightly floured surface. Cover; let rest for 10 minutes. Meanwhile, lightly grease an 8×4×2-inch loaf pan.

Shape dough into a loaf by patting or rolling. To shape by patting, gently pat and pinch dough into an 8-inch-long loaf, tucking edges underneath. To shape by rolling, on a lightly floured surface roll dough into a 12×8-inch rectangle. Roll up rectangle, starting from a short side. Seal seams by pinching dough with your fingertips.

Place shaped dough into prepared pan. Cover and let rise in a warm place until dough is nearly double in size (30 to 40 minutes).

Preheat oven to 350°F. Bake for 35 to 40 minutes or until bread sounds hollow when lightly tapped. If necessary to prevent overbrowning, cover bread loosely with foil during the last 10 minutes of baking. Immediately remove bread from pan. Cool on a wire rack.

In a Twinkling
Disk Disguises

▼ Jolly Takeout

A holiday take-out container is a fun way to give a CD or DVD. Line the container with tissue paper; tuck in some candy canes and the disc. To protect the disc, place it in a sleeve or plastic case before packaging.

Under Wraps

A cloth napkin wraps a disc in style. Secure the wrap in place with a Christmas pin.

So Ornamental ▶

Here's a great idea for guest favors. Back discs with printed paper trimmed slightly larger than discs using decorative-edge scissors. Cut a hole in the center of the paper and thread a chenille stem through the paper and the disc to make a hanger. Hot-glue a scrapbooking embellishment to the hanger and display the ornaments on a tree. When guests choose a CD, be sure to send them home with the matching case.

INSPIRE *the* KIDS

From gifts to make to ideas for trimming their rooms for holiday guests, kids will find oodles of inspiration in this craft-it-yourself chapter.

Room to Bloom

Pom-Pom Fringes

■ Create a sense of fantasy with a see-through wall of fluffy polka dots.

What You'll Need

- [ ] orange yarn
- [ ] scissors
- [ ] large-eye embroidery needle
- [ ] pom-poms in assorted sizes and colors
- [ ] ½-inch-wide ribbon the width of the doorway in the color of the doorway
- [ ] adhesive hook-and-loop dots, squares, or strips

1 Cut the yarn into 5 lengths, each the same height as the doorway. Thread the needle with 1 length of yarn. Stitch through the center of a pom-pom. Pull the pom-pom down the length of yarn. Thread the next pom-pom, pulling it down the yarn, leaving 1½ inches between the first and second pom-pom. Continue threading on pom-poms, leaving equal space between them. Repeat for each yarn length.

2 Sew the yarn lengths, evenly spaced, along the ribbon. Knot the ends to secure. Attach the ribbon to the top of the doorway using the adhesive pieces.

Fancy That

■ It's amazing what a strand of feather boa can do. Simply hot-glue a length around the edge of a mirror for girly girls. For young lads, try rubber snakes, thick jute rope, or sports stickers.

Basket Full of Posies

■ Rim a handy basket with pretty posies or any desired motif. Use foam-flower stickers to hold ribbon stems in place, allowing the tails to blow in the breeze. Dot the center of each flower with a foam circle.

BFF Frame

Display a pic of your best buddy by crafting a cheery picture frame that is crazy with color and shining with sentiment. Choose a photo frame with flat sides to make embellishing a breeze. Start by adhering bands of ribbon on opposite sides as shown. Complete the frame by adhering the letter tiles in place and finish by filling in the spaces with dimensional stickers. This style of frame can be customized for anyone by simply changing the frame color, words, and sticker theme.

Fun and Funky Ornaments

■ Let the tree steal the show with festive ornaments the whole family will enjoy making. Punch various shapes from double-sided scrapbook papers and curl the edges. Use colorful straight pins to attach the shapes to foam balls, piercing through button holes, if desired, and then through the centers of paper shapes. A ribbon bow and loop top each ornament.

Notes of Thanks

■ Have fun creating thank-you cards to send to everyone who gave you a present. Gather up scrapbook papers, cardstock, glue sticks, and alphabet stickers and let the fun begin. Learn how to say "thank you" in several languages.

Paper Potpourri

Make a big impact with easy-to-make decorations and thank-you cards crafted from pretty papers in all your favorite colors.

Playful Pet Boxes

Perfect to make as party favors or as small gift holders, these puppy and kitty boxes are adorable and super fun to make!

Ruff and Meow

■ Craft cuddly creatures of all sorts to trim small cardboard boxes. Use your imagination to design other animals, such as pigs, rabbits, and raccoons. The fun boxes make great organizers as well as gifts for family, friends, and teachers.

What You'll Need

- ☐ tracing paper
- ☐ pencil
- ☐ scissors
- ☐ oval cardboard box
- ☐ glue stick
- ☐ scrapbook papers in 2 coordinating prints
- ☐ black cardstock
- ☐ decorative-edge scissors
- ☐ large paper punch

1 Trace the desired dog and/or cat pattern pieces on page 157; cut them out. Draw around the patterns on scrapbook papers and cardstock; cut out as in Photo A.

2 On scrapbook paper trace around the box lid as shown in Photo B; cut out shape and glue to box lid.

3 Glue the ear shapes to black cardstock; trim around the shapes with decorative-edge scissors as shown in Photo C.

4 Punch 2 circles from black for the eyes as shown in Photo D.

5 Cut nose, whiskers, and eye ring from black cardstock as shown in Photo E.

6 Use glue stick to adhere the ears and other details to the lid, using the photo as a guide for placement.

Bank On It

Create piggy banks for yourself and your friends. While the flower motifs work well for girls, boys will appreciate car, star, or sports ball shapes.

Petunia Piggy

■ Give a piggy bank a cool coat with some simple techniques that turn plain into blooms with bling.

- plain white piggy bank, available in crafts stores
- paintbrushes in fan and small round styles
- glass paint, such as Liquitex Glossies, in light and dark pink, white, and purple
- pencil with new eraser
- adhesive acrylic gems

1 Wash and dry the piggy bank.

2 Using the fan brush and light pink paint, "dust" the surface of the bank with Xs to give the surface texture while allowing the white of the bank to show through as shown in Photo A. Let the paint dry.

3 For large flowers, dip the pencil eraser into paint and dot in a small circle on bank as shown in Photo B. Wash off the eraser before changing colors. Let the paint dry.

4 For the small flowers, paint petals and dot centers using the small round paintbrush as shown in Photo C; let the paint dry.

5 Press adhesive acrylic gems in the centers of the large flowers. You can match the colors or use gems in colors that contrast the paint.

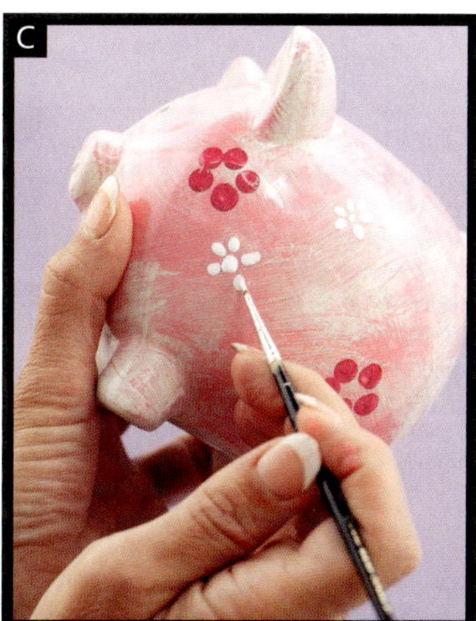

In a Twinkling
Bejeweled Trims

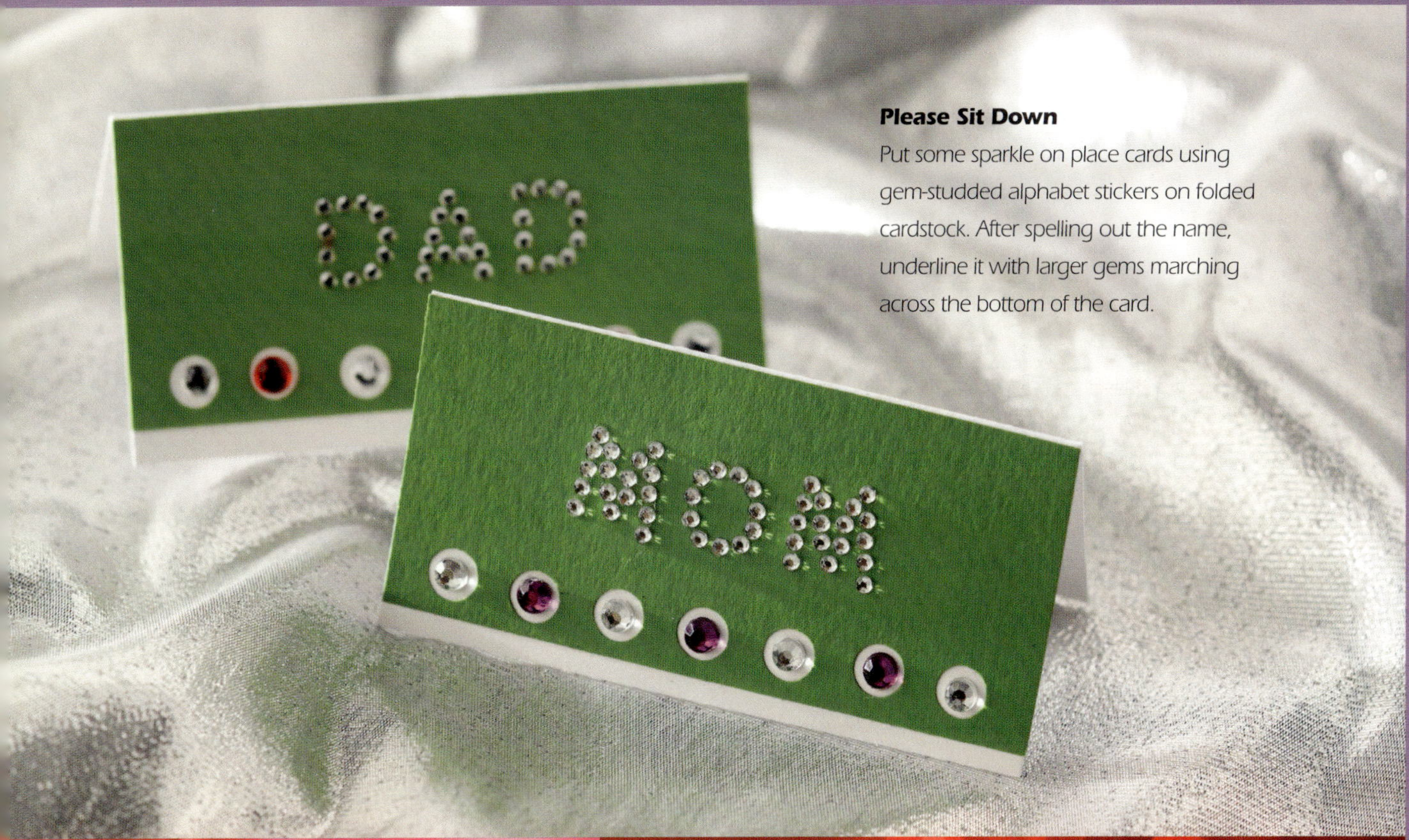

Please Sit Down

Put some sparkle on place cards using gem-studded alphabet stickers on folded cardstock. After spelling out the name, underline it with larger gems marching across the bottom of the card.

Fire Ring ▲

Set a silver napkin ring ablaze with gems in vivid reds and pinks. For a dramatic impact, cluster the gems on one side of the ring, leaving narrow spaces between them.

No Two Alike ▶

Arrange gems in symmetrical patterns on votive holders and they appear as snowflakes glistening in the light. For added dimension, layer with smaller gems.

Patterns

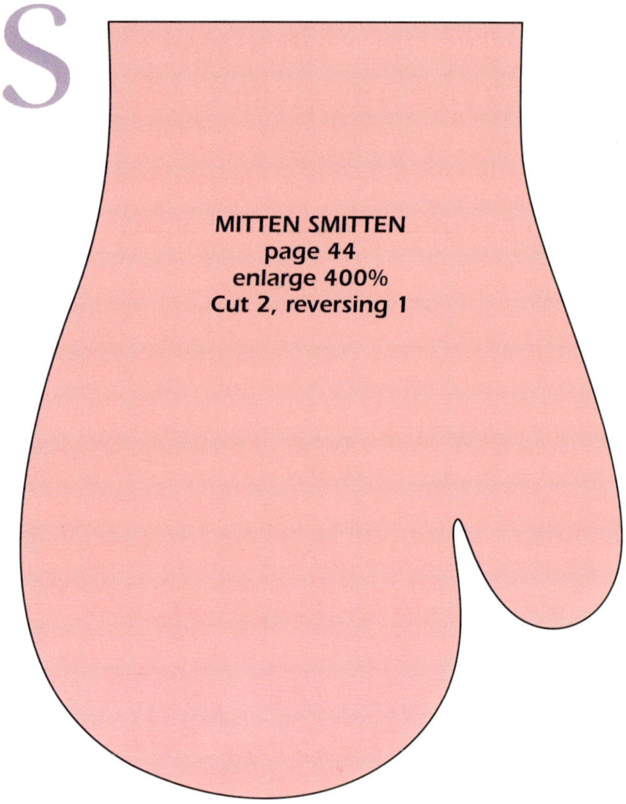

MITTEN SMITTEN
page 44
enlarge 400%
Cut 2, reversing 1

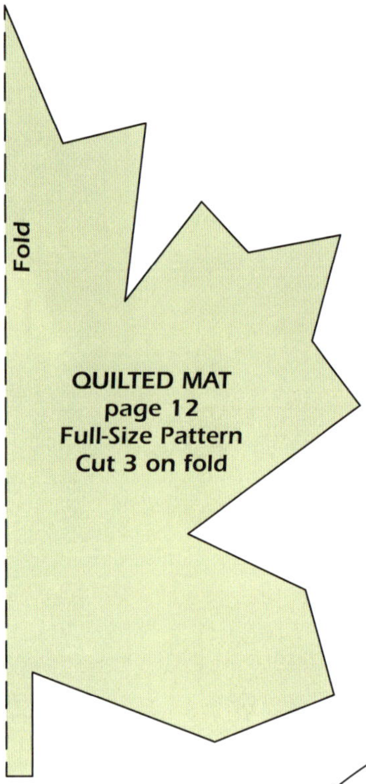

Fold

QUILTED MAT
page 12
Full-Size Pattern
Cut 3 on fold

PIECED PRETTIES
LARGE CIRCLE
page 38
Full-Size Pattern
Trim scalloped edge
as shown on page 38.

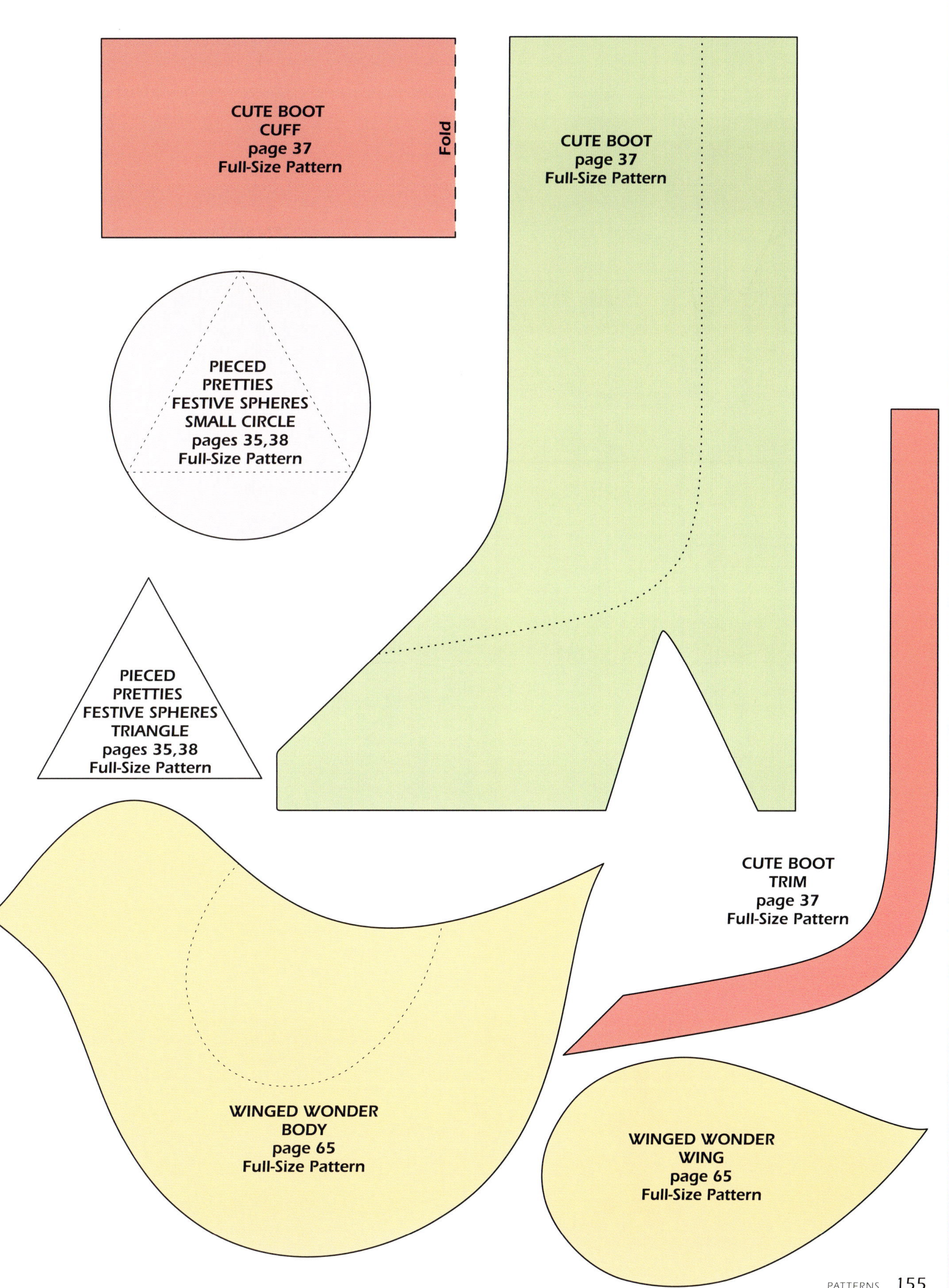

CUTE BOOT
CUFF
page 37
Full-Size Pattern
Fold
CUTE BOOT
page 37
Full-Size Pattern
PIECED
PRETTIES
FESTIVE SPHERES
SMALL CIRCLE
pages 35,38
Full-Size Pattern
PIECED
PRETTIES
FESTIVE SPHERES
TRIANGLE
pages 35,38
Full-Size Pattern
CUTE BOOT
TRIM
page 37
Full-Size Pattern
WINGED WONDER
BODY
page 65
Full-Size Pattern
WINGED WONDER
WING
page 65
Full-Size Pattern

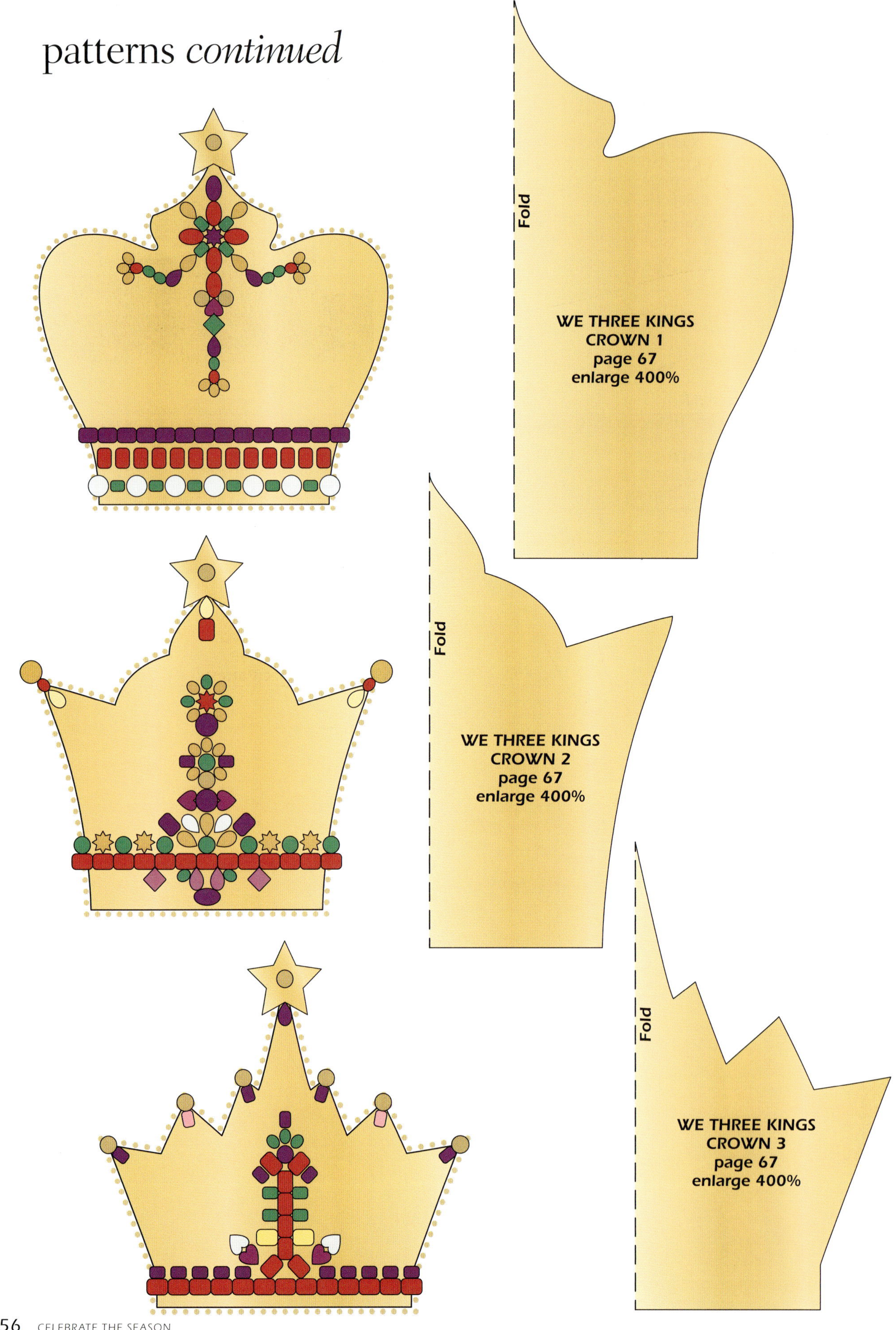
WE THREE KINGS
CROWN 1
page 67
enlarge 400%
Fold

WE THREE KINGS
CROWN 2
page 67
enlarge 400%
Fold

WE THREE KINGS
CROWN 3
page 67
enlarge 400%
Fold

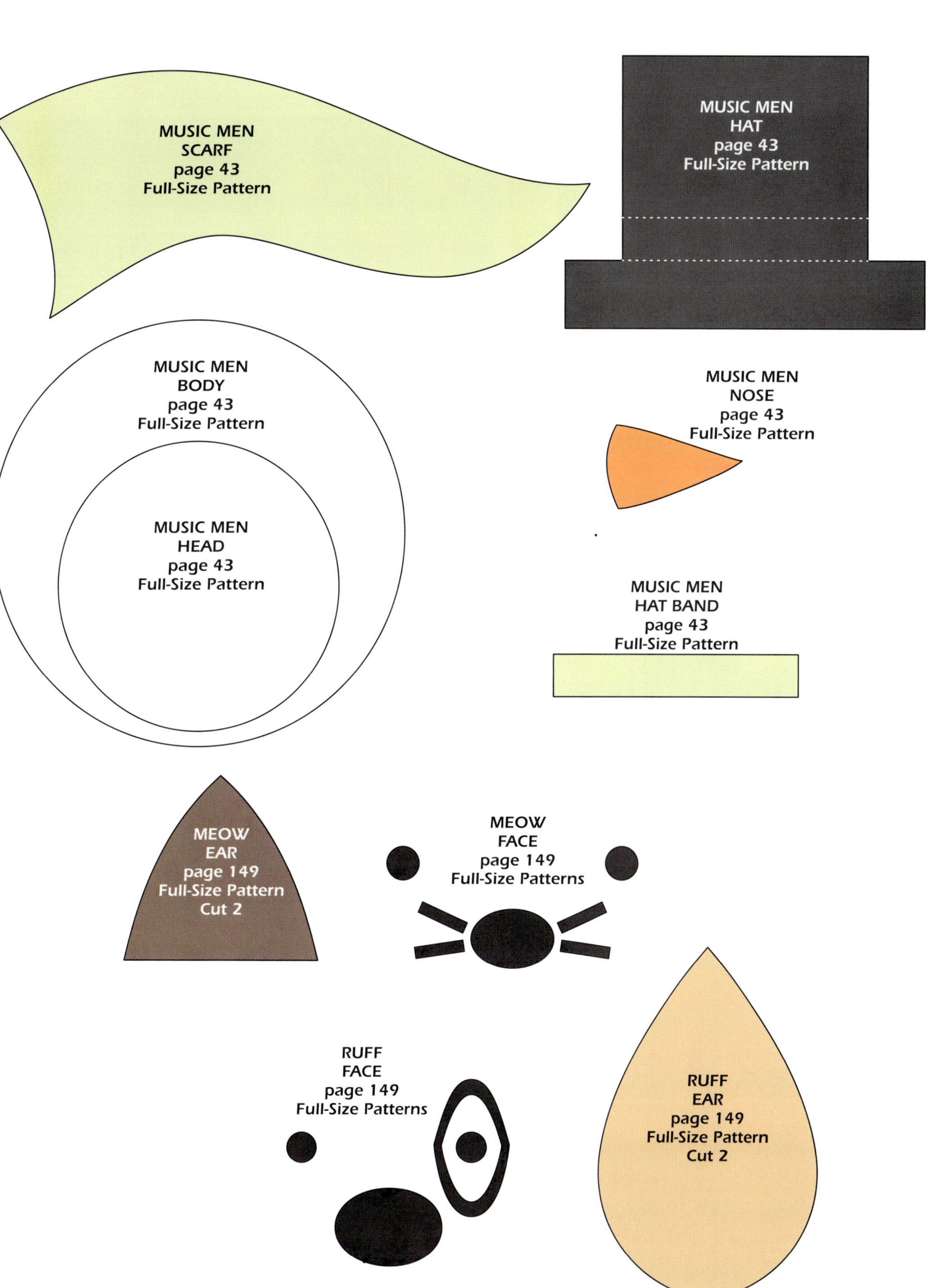

MUSIC MEN
SCARF
page 43
Full-Size Pattern

MUSIC MEN
HAT
page 43
Full-Size Pattern

MUSIC MEN
BODY
page 43
Full-Size Pattern

MUSIC MEN
HEAD
page 43
Full-Size Pattern

MUSIC MEN
NOSE
page 43
Full-Size Pattern

MUSIC MEN
HAT BAND
page 43
Full-Size Pattern

MEOW
EAR
page 149
Full-Size Pattern
Cut 2

MEOW
FACE
page 149
Full-Size Patterns

RUFF
FACE
page 149
Full-Size Patterns

RUFF
EAR
page 149
Full-Size Pattern
Cut 2

patterns *continued*

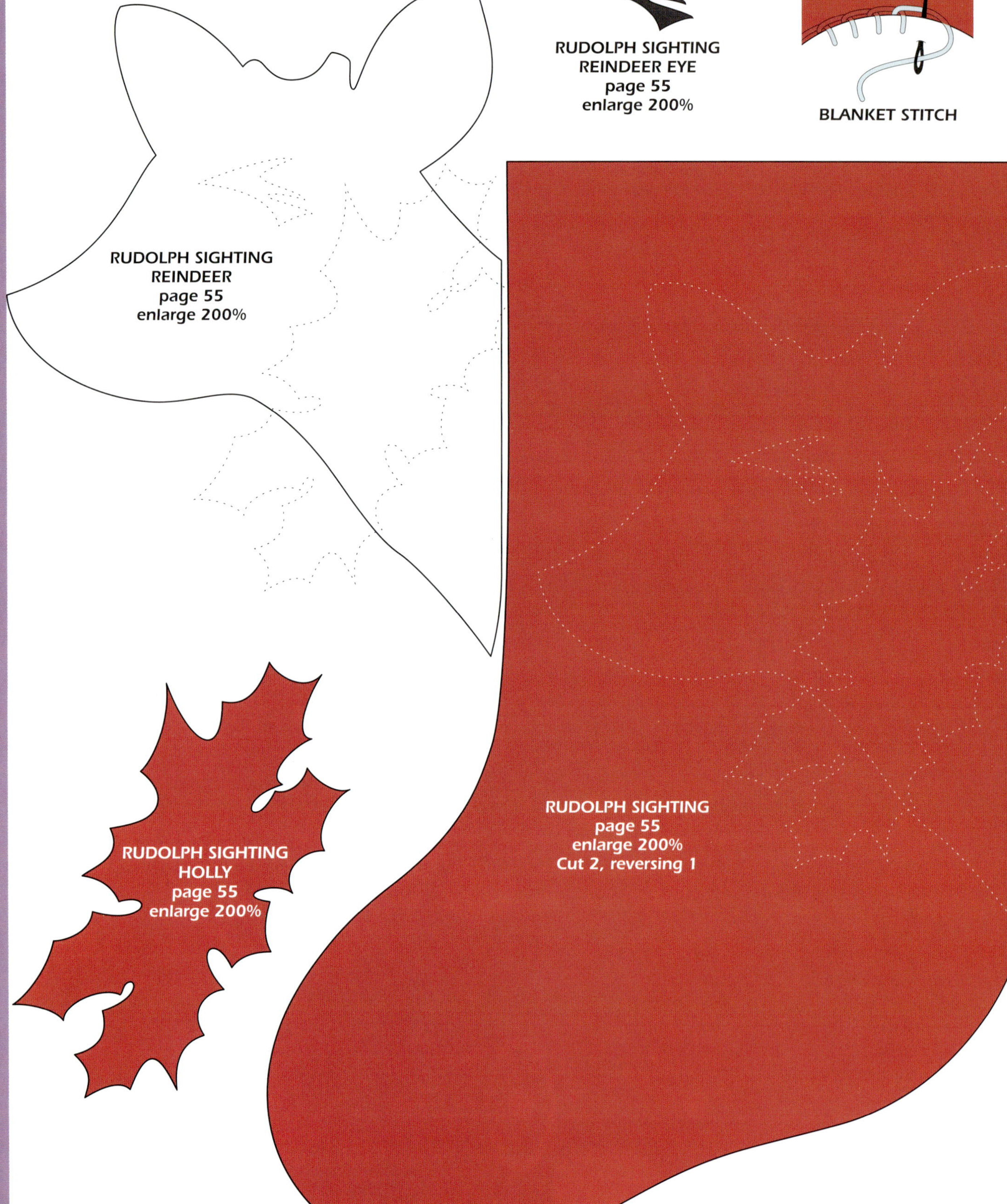

Index

index *continued*

CREDITS & SOURCES

PHOTO STYLING
Sue Banker and Catherine Brett

PHOTOGRAPHY
Jason Donnelly
Scott Little
Kritsada Panichgul
Jay Wilde

FOOD STYLISTS
Dianna Nolan
Jennifer Peterson

PROJECT DESIGNS
Sue Banker

SOURCES
Page 10 – Copper acrylic paint by Plaid Enterprises, Inc., PO Box 7600, Norcross, GA 30091-7600; plaidonline.com.

Pages 18–19 – Glaze by General Finishes, 2462 Corporate Circle, East Troy, WI 53120; sales@generalfinishes.com; 800/783-6050.

Pages 57, 127 – Etching cream by Armour Products, 176-180 5th Avenue, Hawthorne, NJ 07506.

Pages 68–69 – Sculpey oven-bake clay by Polyform Products Company, 1901 Estes Avenue, Elk Grove Village, IL 60007-5415; info@polyformproducts.com.

Pages 68–69 – Gold acrylic paint by Plaid Enterprises, Inc., PO Box 7600, Norcross, GA 30091-7600; plaidonline.com.

Pages 70–71 – Acrylic paints in gold, bronze, and black by Plaid Enterprises, Inc., PO Box 7600, Norcross, GA 30091-7600; plaidonline.com.

Pages 80–85 – Acrylic paints by Plaid Enterprises, Inc., PO Box 7600, Norcross, GA 30091-7600; plaidonline.com.

SPECIAL THANKS TO
Kidman Tree Farm, 3665 NW 98th Avenue, Polk City, IA 50226.